C000179846

Table of Contents

Chapter 1: Introduction

"I always wonder why the birds stay in the same place when they can fly anywhere on the earth. Then I ask myself the same question" - Harun Yahya

A slave, born into slavery, cannot contemplate the existence of freedom. Most slaves won't even know that they are born slaves. Without that awareness a slave will never make conscious efforts to free himself. Someone has to purposefully make him aware of his existential reality. Only when he is made aware of this fact can he can start thinking about freedom. And if he is enlightened enough, he can work towards his emancipation, and finally attain his freedom.

Many of us think that we are free souls, or at least we would like to see ourselves as one. However, the sad truth is that the majority of us are slaves to a system we are born into. We are simply not aware of it. It is not exactly physical slavery, but more of mental slavery. And because we are not aware of it, we do not endeavor to find our way out of this slavery. However, the good news is that once you are aware of it doesn't take much time to get out of it.

When I set out to write this book, my main aspiration was to make you aware of the slavery system we are born into and show you the way to freedom by developing new ways of thinking. This is important mainly because the man who is not able to develop and use his mind is bound to be a slave of the other man who can better use his mind. Though freedom may mean different things to different people, the kind of freedom we will be referring to in this book is specifically 'financial freedom'. So, throughout this book, the terms freedom and financial freedom will be used interchangeably.

In today's socio-economic world money equals freedom. However, most of us are not aware of this fact. This is the reason why so many of us end up working for money our entire life, instead of learning how to make money work for us. And to make more money most people simply work more hours. Even people who already have enough money keep on working for more money, not necessarily because they enjoy the work they do, but mainly because they think that more money will bring more happiness or solve all their problems.

Money has become the master and men the slaves, instead of the other way around. It is always either of these two: Man is the master and money the slave, or money is the master and man the slave. No one is neutral with money. Anyone who says that he or she is neutral with money is either a liar or an ascetic living in some caves in the Himalayas.

My aim here is to help you become the master of money and make money your slave. It is only when you become a master of money that you will be able to gain your financial freedom. The more money you can convert into your slaves the more quickly you will be able to gain your freedom. When you are the master of money it will come to you easily and effortlessly. It will come to you frequently and in increasing quantities. It will come to you in miraculous ways, and from different sources - both from known sources as well as unknown sources.

Money can work for you continuously, day-in and day-out, and bring you more money.

This book is not about saying 'Time is money'. Rather it is about saying 'Money is time'. It is about making and accumulating money to free up more of your time, and your life. Ultimately the goal is to help you accumulate enough money which generates enough passive incomes to cover your day-to-day expenses. This is the point which I want you to reach. This is your financial freedom point.

As a disclaimer, this book is not intended for people who already have attained their financial freedom or people who are already rich beyond their wildest dreams. This book is also not a guide on how to pick stocks or which property to buy. This book is also not intended to make you extremely wealthy. There are also no 'get rich quick schemes' and 'no overnight success formulas' prescribed in this book.

This book is intended mainly for people who are still stuck in the rat-race, living paycheck to paycheck, who are slaves to money, and want to find their freedom. It is for people who are willing to free themselves from the shackles of financial worries. It is for people who want to attain financial freedom and do whatever they want and whenever they want. It is for people who want to work for the love of the work and not for the money. It is an endeavor to take you from where you are now to the point of your financial freedom. Once you reach this point it is all up to you to become extremely wealthy if you want to. You can now work for joy and not for money.

This book also intends to bring about a paradigm shift in your thought patterns. It believes that money is a game and will strive to make you a better player and increases your chances of winning this game. It will also help you demystify some of the self-defeating beliefs about money.

After reading this book you will be set on your path to attaining your financial freedom. If you stick to some of the 'gaps' mentioned in this book and put them into practice you can attain your financial freedom in just 3-5 years, depending on the level of your commitment and the number of 'gaps' you can put into practice. Always remember that the 'gaps' have a multiplicative effect. The more 'gaps' you can put into practice the sooner you will attain your freedom.

This book will enable you to improve some of your daily money habits and make your journey towards your financial freedom faster. These are not radical changes that will drastically distort the harmony in your life. Instead, they are tiny little adjustments here and there that will have a huge impact over a long period. As Aristotle put it, **"We are what we repeatedly do. Excellence, then, is not an act but a habit."** The best way to make personal improvement is to create small but progressive daily wins consistently.

This book will travel along with you to your path of financial freedom. It will serve as your tour guide. It will bid farewell and wish you all the best once you reach your financial freedom. If getting rich is your goal it is up to you to attain it from thereon. I can guarantee you that the road to becoming rich is more realistic and more easily attainable once you are financially free.

Unlike the old saying **"Give a man a fish and he will be dependent on you. Teach him to fish and he is set for life"**, this book is not just about teaching you how to fish. Rather it is to enlighten you that there are many ways of catching fish. It is to illuminate you that you can also catch fish without your active engagement, even while you are asleep. It is only when you learn how to catch fishes while you are asleep that you will attain your true freedom. You can stop trading your time for the fishes and still get enough fishes to sustain your life. However, if fishing is what you love doing you can do it for the love of it. You can now fish for joy and not because you have to. When you go fishing for the joy of it you will end up catching more fish.

Many people focus only on making money. However, wealthy people focus on building and creating systems that can make money. Though the distinction between the two is little it can make a huge difference. One can keep you poor or middle class for the rest of your life, the other can make you rich and free.

Once you learned how to catch fishes without being actively engaged in the process you can catch as many fishes as you want by simply replicating the process. This is called leverage. However, you will have to invest your time and energy into building the system. It will also take lots of effort and sacrifice. But once you have a system in place, to catch enough fish to sustain you and your family, you are free. That's your freedom.

Research has shown that making more money makes a person happier, but only up to a certain point. Beyond that point, what economists call 'diminishing marginal returns' sets in, and more money stops making you happier. This is because money, only up to a certain level, is a need. Beyond that point, they are just numbers. To me, money is a need for attaining one's financial freedom.

So, in a nutshell the cornerstone of this book is not really in the money itself, but rather in the freedom that the money can buy. Money is a tool and is a very important one. It will be your friend, your servant, and your loyal slave who will willfully work for you when you are awake or when you are asleep, and help you attain your freedom, and continue to keep you free in the future as well.

This book is about doing the things that your future self would love to come back to this present moment and thank you for doing those tiny little adjustments in your day-to-day life that ultimately resulted in your freedom. It is about doing what is significant as soon as possible and achieving your financial freedom as quickly as possible.

This book will take you through nine different 'gaps' that will help you attain your financial freedom faster. These 'gaps' are the tiny little adjustments that you make now, about the way you think or act, that will eventually make a huge difference later on in your life. They are the minute alterations, in your daily thought patterns and habits. Most people are not even aware of the existence of such gaps. This book is all about what those gaps are and how to find your way to financial freedom through those gaps. One gap alone can help you attain your financial freedom. However, as mentioned earlier the gaps have a multiplicative effect. So, the more gaps you can combine the faster you will reach your financial freedom.

Chapter 2: The Money Paradigm

The Psychology of Money

How we were brought up as a child greatly influences how we think and behave as adults. We were all introduced to the subject of money at some point in our lives. Most of the statements we heard about money growing up - from our parents, our schools, our societies, or the people we hang around with - remain lodged deep inside our subconscious mind as our money-paradigms. Though these paradigms are unconscious beliefs about money, they drive most of our thoughts and behaviors about money for the rest of our lives. They ultimately shape our financial health. Also, as these paradigms are passed-on from generation-to-generation, they tend to stay with us for the rest of our life unless we intentionally make efforts to change them. Many of us are not even aware that most of our financial decisions are run automatically by our money-paradigms.

Someone once said, **"If you took all the money in the world and divide it equally among everybody, it would soon be back in the same pockets it was before"**. It is because, when it comes to money, most of us are hardwired to act and behave in predictable ways through our money-paradigms. These money-paradigms are like the thermostat of our financial temperature. They will always take us to the amount of money that we unconsciously set in our subconscious mind. These money-paradigms are also somewhat like a container in our subconscious mind. We can only retain that amount of money that we can comfortably hold within this container. Jim Rohn once said, **"If someone hands you a million dollars, best you become a millionaire, or you won't get to keep the money."** To be a millionaire is about the money-paradigm, not about the million dollars. If someone hands you a million dollars and if your money-paradigm is conditioned to contain only a few thousand dollars, you will soon end up spending all your money unnecessarily until you are left with a few thousand dollars. The rest will simply overflow. Similarly, if your money-paradigm is conditioned to contain only a few thousand dollars your subconscious mind will find a way to generate those few thousand dollars even when you are broke.

Your money-paradigm greatly determines your financial success or the amount of wealth you can accumulate. You can acquire all the knowledge and skills in the world, but if you prime your money-paradigm for failure, you cannot be financially successful. If your money-paradigm is non-supportive to your financial success, you will automatically make poor financial choices that are detrimental to your success, without you even realizing it. Conversely, if you condition your money-paradigm for financial success, you will automatically make decisions that produce success. You won't even have to think about it. It will be your habitual way of thinking.

Most people are poor because they are not aware of the fact that their non-supportive money-paradigms are making most of their financial decisions. It is for this reason that many talented individuals and professionals are struggling financially. There are also lots of individuals who made tons of money but ended up bankrupt. Research has also shown that most lottery winners eventually return to their original financial state. They go back to the same amount of money they can comfortably handle according to their money-paradigms.

However, the good thing about the money-paradigm is that they are changeable. No matter where you are in the evolution of your money paradigm, you can continue to improve and progress.

How to Change Your Money-Paradigm?

"The unexamined life is not worth living." – Socrates

The first element of all changes is awareness. Awareness is the best starting point for making any changes and improving your overall financial health. You can't change something unless you know it exists. You can gain awareness about your money-paradigm by examining your family background and your environmental exposure as a child. What did your parents, teachers, friends, and society teach you about money? Reflect on them.

By identifying your money-paradigm and where they came from, you will start gaining power over your relationship with money. Examine both your conscious as well as your unconscious beliefs about money. Evaluate whether your beliefs about money are helping you or are self-sabotaging you. Observe your thoughts, your fears, your habits, your actions, and even your inactions about money. Reflect on and acknowledge your deepest beliefs and values about money.

Bring out everything that you lodge in your subconscious mind into your consciousness. It will not be easy at first, but with regular practice, you'll soon become an expert at it. Create a ritual around becoming aware and reviewing your financial situation. You'll be in a much better position to make conscious choices about what wealth means to you. You can begin to evolve and move forward and create a life in which you can prosper.

To bring about positive changes in our relationship with money, we must become conscious of our true desires and make decisions. We must make decisions that serve us rather than drive us. When it comes to money, it is often our misunderstanding of reality that hurts us. Most of us are living in a la-la-land when it comes to the subject of money.

Consciousness is a critical step in making constructive changes in your subconscious money-paradigm. Observing your thoughts and actions can help you live in the present moment and help you make decisions that serve you rather than cripple you. It can stop your past programming to command your life. Consciousness is having a clear picture of who you are, where you came from, and where you want to go. Without that awareness, life can become an endless pattern of unconscious repetition. To be financially successful, you must learn to live consciously. The habit of consciousness is the key to turn even the direst situations into prosperity. Consciously approaching our finances is the key.

"We cannot solve our problems with the same thinking we used when we created them." —Albert Einstein

Scientific study shows that our subconscious mind is about 90 percent of the mind. And the subconscious mind is what shapes our money paradigm. We can change our money paradigm by priming our subconscious mind. We can feed it with new information and statements about money. We can do this by engaging ourselves in repetitive positive affirmations about money. We can engage in positive self-talk about money. These are the processes of making investments into your subconscious mind. Investing in your subconscious mind will always give you compounding returns. Whatever you deposit in your subconscious mind gets magnified and multiplied many times. The subconscious mind operates in an auto-pilot mode. It maneuvers your life as per the conditionings it gets. It is the silent pilot of your life. Yet, you can train your subconscious mind to attract whatever you desire in life.

What Is Money?

The meanings we attribute to money can be different. Money is something that we use every day. We earn it and spend it but don't often think much about it. One can either have a healthy relationship or a bad relationship with money. To have a healthy relationship with the money, one must know what money is. People spend their entire life chasing money without actually knowing what it represents.

Money is like a catalyst. You may recall from your chemistry class that a catalyst speeds up a chemical reaction. Yet, the catalyst itself does not get consumed in the process. Likewise, money has no value in and of itself but acts as a stimulus through its exchange value. It derives its value from its purchasing power. It also acts as a storage of value, which is exchangeable for goods and services. It makes trading of one product to another easy. Money can also act as a lubricant in your financial life. It enables you to slide through life instead of having to scrape by.

Money is also rightly called currency. To survive and thrive, you must learn to be better conductors of money. Money is a form of energy and must always be in motion. The more money flows through you the more financial power you can exert. You can in turn become a powerful transformer for your family and the society through properly channelizing the power of money.

Money is important because it has the power to buy what we want and to enjoy the finer things in life. Most important of all, money has the power to bring freedom to do what you want with your time and energy. Knowing that you are free to choose what to do with your life is not only financially advantageous but also psychologically empowering.

The Power of Choices

"The reason man may become the master of his own destiny is because he has the power to influence his own subconscious mind." - Napoleon Hill

You are at the steering wheel of your financial life, through the power of choices. We have the freedom to choose which thoughts to entertain and which thoughts to discard. You can always choose to think in ways that will support you in your happiness and success, or in ways that will sabotage you. Your thoughts and feelings control your destinies.

One Native American parable, about an old Cherokee teaching his grandson about life, nicely captures the importance of how our personal choices shape our lives. He said **"A terrible fight is going on inside me between two wolves. One of the wolves is evil - he is angry, envious, jealous, sorrowful, greedy, arrogant, vengeful, and violent. The other is good - he is generous, joyful, peaceful, loving, compassionate, hopeful, humble, and kind."** The grandson thought about it for a minute and then asked his grandfather **"Which wolf will win?"** The old Cherokee simply replied, **"Whichever one I feed."**

The same fight is going on inside each of us. It is really up to us to decide which wolf will win the fight within us. Whatever thoughts we focus our attention on is what we are feeding. What we focus on is what grows and becomes our reality through our thoughts, feelings, and actions.

In life, we might not always be in a position to choose the circumstances that we are in, but we can always choose the way we respond to them. According to Viktor Frankl, the celebrated Austrian psychiatrist and a holocaust survivor (who was a prisoner in Nazi concentration camps during World War II), the meaning in life does not come from what happens to us, but from how we interpret what happens to us, and how we respond to it. When faced with challenges in life we can feel victimized and give others power over our lives, or we can take personal responsibility for the choices that we make. It is our responses to life's challenges that ultimately determine our level of prosperity and the richness of our lives.

Our intentions also play an important role in shaping our financial lives. What is happening in our lives are just reflections of what is going on inside our mind. The reason we have for making money is vital. If the motivation for acquiring money comes from non-supportive thoughts, then money will never bring us happiness. For instance, if you save money for some rainy-days your primary focus is on the rainy-days and rainy-days is what you will get. However, if you shift your reason for saving money to, say achieving financial freedom, that is exactly what you will get. Same action, different intentions, different results.

Today, when it comes to money, many people are driven by fear rather than by abundance thinking. They fear that they won't have enough money to carry them through an uncertain future. Fear in itself is constrictive and disempowering. It can feed on itself, and it rarely leads to balanced and constructive decisions. Allowing fear to keep us from spending money is certainly counterproductive for creating prosperity. Wealth is about having a life of purpose and being able to fulfill that purpose.

The Money-Paradigms of The Rich and The Poor

One of the reasons why the rich are getting richer and the poor stay poor is because of their money-paradigms. There is a huge difference between the money-paradigms of the rich as compared to that of the poor and middle-class. Rich people always think abundance and thereby attract more and more riches of all kinds. The poor and middle-class, on the other hand, constantly think of lack and have a hard time attracting riches to their lives. Rich people have clear goals, unwavering desire, and are fully committed to creating wealth. Poor and middle-class people are not. Rich people also learned how to make their money work for them while the poor and middle-class people work hard for money their entire life. What you think is what you are, and what you believe is what you're going to have. You can choose to think and act like the rich people and therefore create the results that rich people create.

Financial Freedom Through Passive Income

Most people have money-paradigms that are set only for earning active incomes as against earning passive incomes. As a result, most people work hard for money but end up spending all their money, which results in their having to work hard forever. Working hard is important but working hard alone will never make you rich enough to be financially free. You must work hard for money but at the same time, you must also learn how to invest your money.

When you invest your money, it works hard for you instead of you working hard for the money. Every dollar you earn ca be treated like a seed that can be planted to earn hundreds of dollars, which can then be replanted to earn thousands of dollars. Every dollar you spend today may actually cost you hundreds and thousands of dollars tomorrow. Always remember whenever you are spending money you are spending a portion of your potential future freedom.

Also working hard for money can be made a temporary situation. You can work hard until your money works hard enough to take your place. The more money you can put to work for you, the less you will need to work. First, you work hard for the money, then you let the money work hard for you.

The achieve your financial-freedom you must create a financial-freedom fund as soon as possible. Think of this fund as the goose that lays the golden eggs. These golden eggs are your passive incomes. The money accumulated in this fund is never to be spent. Even the interests earned, and dividends received are to be reinvested. It is only meant for investments to ultimately bring you financial freedom by generating enough passive incomes to cover your expenses. Eventually, when you attain your financial freedom you can spend some of the incomes (the golden eggs) from this fund, but never deplete the accumulated fund (the golden goose). Once the financial-freedom fund is big enough it will also feed on itself.

Attaining your financial freedom is also more than just about being wealthy. It is a true sign of control over your life. Unless you can eliminate your need for money, you have to figure out a way to control it, or it will control you. Either you control your money, or your money will control you. And to control your money, you must learn to manage it.

It's not just about what comes in, it's about what you do with what comes in. It doesn't matter if you have a fortune right now or virtually nothing. What matters is that you immediately begin to manage what you've got. The habit of managing your money is more important than the amount itself. Money is a big part of your life, and when you learn how to get your finances under control, all other areas of your life will soar along with it. Also having the freedom to apply your attention, energy, and love to an endeavor of your choosing is a gift that you will have earned well when it arrives. It's about having the freedom and the ability to do things you can't otherwise do.

Importance of Education

"If you think education is expensive, try ignorance." - Benjamin Franklin

In life, if you don't know where you want to go - if you are unconscious of what you want - ending up "somewhere else" may be the inevitable result. Unconscious decisions and a lack of information are affecting many young people today. Unless you are willing to expand your financial comfort zone you will stay stuck exactly where you are. However, education and information can make all the difference.

People can make good financial decisions when they have the information they need and when they understand what it takes to achieve their financial goals. Your comfort level talking about your money will also increase with the increase in your financial knowledge.

One of my favorite sayings about the importance of educating oneself is by the author and philosopher Eric Hoffer, who said, **"The learners shall inherit the earth while the learned will be beautifully equipped to live in a world that no longer exists."** It's important to continually build upon that foundation.

As you progress through your financial education and wealth-building journey, your mindset too will evolve. Embrace those changes but be sure to constantly evaluate them and make sure that they align with what your financial goals are.

Building wealth is more than just about taking specific actions. It is about changing our mindset and lifestyle. Wealth itself is a fluid concept. Our view of the good life has changed and evolved around the world, which is good news for us as individuals. If the definition of wealth is changeable, it implies that we have the opportunity to discover and define what wealth means to us personally and to take steps to achieve it. At the same time always remember that it is not the pursuit of wealth that brings meaning and value to life. Rather, it is the pursuit of meaning and value that brings wealth.

The Greatest Secret

The greatest secret in the world is that the answers to all our problems are locked within our subconscious mind. It is our responsibility to unlock those secrets through conscious efforts. People can change and become better if they choose to. Our old ways of thinking and acting have gotten us exactly where we are right now. And the first step toward changing our old way of thinking is to identify them. If you want to move to a higher level of life, you have to be willing to replace some of your old ways of thinking with new ones.

Also, you can only decide on what actions you'll need to take to achieve your goals only when you are aware of your goals. It is only when you know what prosperity means to you personally that you can start to move toward it. It is only when you know this that you can begin to make conscious choices that lead to better financial destinies. You can choose to run your thoughts and not let your thoughts run you. You can choose to be the captain of your ship.

The number one reason why most people don't get what they want in life is that they don't know what they want. Most people who choose to get paid for your time are pretty much killing their chances of building wealth. For the most part, they end up buying things for immediate gratification in a futile attempt to make up for their dissatisfaction in life.

To achieve anything worthwhile requires that we take some chances and be willing to move out of our comfort zone. People who achieve true prosperity let neither risk nor setbacks stop them. If you are not fully, totally, and truly committed to creating wealth, chances are you won't.

You must also grow your subconscious mind to be a big container of wealth so that it can, not only hold more wealth but also attract more wealth. The universe abhors a vacuum and if you have a very large money container, it will rush in to fill the space.

Money is something that people use every day. We earn it and spend it but don't often think much about it.

Chapter 3: The Goal- Financial Freedom

There is a saying that an average of 3% of all human populations has written goals and the rest 97% work for them. This shows how important goal setting is for your success. All successful people set goals and work towards achieving them. Earl Nightingale said **"Success is nothing more than the progressive realization of a worthy ideal. This means that any person who knows what they are doing and where they are going is a success. Any person with a goal towards which they are working is a successful person."** In other words, people with goals succeed because they know exactly where they are going.

"If a man does not know to which port he is steering, no wind is favorable to him." - Seneca

A ship whose voyage is completely mapped out and planned, and whose captain and crew knows exactly where it is going and how long it will take, will get there 99.99% of the time. This is because it has a definite goal and a concrete plan to achieve that goal. If another similar ship, with no plan and no crew on it, is being made to run with its engine on it will either sink or wind up in some deserted islands. Its chances of randomly reaching any port in the world are almost zero.

Let me illustrate the importance and power of goal setting through the **"Yale University's 1953 Goals Study"**. It goes like this: In 1953, researchers surveyed Yale's graduating seniors to determine how many of them had specific, written goals for their future. The answer: only 3%. Twenty years later the researchers again polled the surviving members of the class of 1953 and found that the 3% with specific, written goals had become much more successful than the rest 97%. These 3% had accumulated more personal financial wealth than the rest 97% combined.

Though there are many attributes of a good goal the main characteristics that I would like to focus on to achieve your financial-freedom goal are as follows.

Specific Goals

Your goals must be specific. If you do not specify your goals it becomes obscure and you will lose your way easily. Your goals are like your guiding stars at night. You must be very thorough about which star to follow and know the star. If you do not specify your goals your subconscious mind will not be able to distinguish what it is that you exactly want to accomplish. So, when you feed your subconscious mind with non-specific goals it will produce results as it deems fit. In a way, our subconscious mind is also like a computer. The quality of output is determined by the quality of the input - Garbage In, Garbage Out.

If you feed your subconscious mind with specific targets it will work towards producing those specific results. However, when you do not specify your goals your subconscious mind gets confused and cannot produce the desired results. Your subconscious mind must be instructed as objectively as possible.

Let us illustrate the importance of specific goals with a few examples. Let us say that your goal goes something like "I want more money", or "I want to be rich". Now, what is more money, or being rich? Is there a universal definition for 'more money' or 'rich'? These are merely subjective statements. More money for one person might be getting another US $100, whereas for another person more money might mean US $1 billion. Being rich for one person might be accumulating US $100,000, while for another person it might mean accumulating US $10 billion or more. If you merely say that you want more money, and not specify the exact amount, your subconscious mind will think that getting another US $100 or US $1,000 is more money. Once it reaches that figure it will stop there, thinking that it has already helped you accomplish your goals.

So, rather than just saying that you want 'more money' you must specify the exact amount of money that you want. You can say something like "I want US $10 million". When you do that your subconscious mind starts registering it. It has a target now and can start working on it. However, there is still one more problem. Your subconscious mind still doesn't know when the US $10 million is to be accumulated. So, you have to specify the timeline as well. You can say "I want US $10 million in my possession by the end of 3 years from now". This is more specific now.

You may notice that I did not specify how we are going to achieve that US $10 million. There is a reason behind it. Too much focus on the 'how' at this stage is not recommendable as it can seem daunting. As stated earlier goal achievement is a process i.e. a path you travel towards your destination. Once you have defined the 'what' of your goal and the 'timeline' for achieving it, your subconscious mind will start working on the 'how' part. If you just have enough faith you can tap into the enormous power of your subconscious mind to help you find your way.

Similarly, rather than just saying "I want to be rich" you can make it more specific by saying "I am planning to accumulate US $100 million in the next 5 years".

Written Goals

Your goals must be written down. There is much more power in written goals as compared to unwritten goals. Written goals are like anchors to your subconscious mind. Also, the moment you write down your goals you become a creator. You have converted what is in your mind into something visible and tangible.

Writing down your goals is also the very first action towards achieving them. You can only achieve your goals through actions, and the moment you write down your goals you have already started taking the first action towards achieving your goal. Remember that what separates you and your goal is the number of actions you are required to take to reach that goal (more on this in the chapter on The Action Gap).

Some of the most successful entrepreneurs are very specific about how they write their goals down. For instance, Grant Cordone, the self-made millionaire and author of the book **'The 10X Rule'** says that he writes down his goals twice a day - once in the morning, and then once again at night. He says **"I want to wake up to it. I want to sleep to it and I want to dream about it. I want to write my goals down before I go to sleep at night because they are important to me, they are valuable to me and I get to wake up to them again tomorrow"**.

A psychology professor Dr. Gail Matthews of the Dominican University in California conducted a study on 'goal setting and writing goals' with 267 participants. In her research, she found out that people with written goals are 42% more likely to achieve them, as compared to those who do not write down their goals.

Active Goals

The more active you are in setting and keeping your goals the higher your chances of success. Goal setting is not a 'do it and forget it' activity. Reaching your goal is not a one-time event. It is a process, with many ups and downs, setbacks, and failures.

The road to success is riddled with many disappointments. You have to always make course corrections along the way. For doing this you have to always reevaluate your progress daily. If you set a worthy enough goal you will never reach, there in a straight line. You will have many setbacks and failures on your path to your financial freedom goal. However, let me also assure you that these setbacks and failures are just a part of the process and you should never be discouraged by them.

There goes an old saying **"To be a champion fight one more round"**. Only tireless pursuits can create winners. Failures are indeed the foundations on which the pillars of success are built. The stronger the foundation the greater the success. You must learn to strive with patience, perseverance, and determination. You have to learn to overcome the hurdles and the obstacles to achieve your goals. With each failure, you get closer to success and with each fall you rise higher because within each failure is hidden a lesson on success. The hurdles and obstacles are there as a filtering device to weed off those individuals who are not determined to achieve their goals.

Research has shown that keeping our focus on the end goal, instead of the traps and pits along the way, will make us more successful in pursuing our goals. This is also what happens when we play videogames. In most videogames, we often encounter setbacks along the way, but we also learn how to tackle them, overcome them, and finally reach our targets. If we can only design our goals like a videogame where there are little concerns for failures our chances of success will be highly enhanced. If we can learn to always focus on the end-goal, and not be disheartened by the intermittent failures along the way, we will also be more motivated to put in more actions. The process will also be fun and more exciting. We can learn to trick our brain into doing things, whose results are not immediate but profound, by making the process more rewarding.

Big Goals

I always believe in setting big, ginormous, and unrealistic goals. Your goals should be intimidating. It should make you feel uncomfortable. There is no power in setting low goals. If your goals are only within your perceived capabilities, you will not be able to grow.

The purpose of setting goals is not to achieve the goals, but to help you grow to become a better person. Throughout history, all great achievements were made by people who refused to be normal. Realistic goals will only make you average. When you set unrealistic goals, you will fail so many times that you will get used to failing and thereby eradicating the 'fear of failure' itself. This will greatly enhance your chances of success. Setting unrealistic goals also pushes you to your limits and forces you to think new ways of looking at the problem at hand. You become more creative in the process.

Financial Freedom Goal

Now that we know a great deal about goal setting let us narrow down your financial freedom goal. Before you start working towards your financial freedom goal you must be very specific about the amount that will make you financially free. Once you come up with that amount you can do some 'back from the future' planning. 'Back from the future planning' is a technique that I used to set timelines for achieving my most important goals. Here, I set some goals to achieve in the future, let's say within 10 years from now. Then I visualize myself already reaching that goal. From there I will mentally come back to the present moment and chart out all the actions that I must do, starting now, to reach where I am 10 years from now. Once all the actions have been specified in detail I will try and complete all the actions in about 3 years. This way I can accelerate my journey towards my financial freedom. Also, if I can accomplish in 3 years, what I had initially intended to accomplish in 10 years, then what I will accomplish in 10 years can be multiples of what I had initially intended.

This financial freedom amount will also vary from person to person. There is no one right amount. If you can maintain a simple lifestyle, with bare minimum necessities, then that figure will be much less, as compared to someone who wants to spend a lavish lifestyle. Whatever lifestyle you chose to live and whatever financial freedom amount you chose to accomplish it is all within your reach. You just

have to decide and be willing to pay the price
for it.

Chapter 4: The Income Gap

Income is the most important component for achieving your financial freedom. It is also the most powerful element in the money-game we all are playing. Money-game is the universal game that we are all required to play by default, like it or not. Everyone is playing this game. One great thing about this money-game is that it is not a zero-sum game. We can all play the game, and all come out as winners. However, unfortunately, many people will never win this game because they don't know what it takes to win this money-game.

All games follow a set of rules which define how the game should be played. These rules are often unwritten but invaluable to the way you play. Most games are also played using strategies. The money-game is no different. To successfully play this money-game one must have a good knowledge of the various components and rules of the game. You must also be able to formulate your strategies for playing the game. However, you can also mimic the strategies of those who have already succeeded. You can get their strategies by reading and doing a little research. That in itself is a very smart strategy. Always remember that success leaves clues. The quickest and easiest way to create wealth is to learn exactly how the rich people, who are masters of money, play the game.

When you start playing the money-game it is common to be rejected by other players early on. Many of the opportunities and tools necessary to successfully play the game will also be locked initially. However, by learning new skills along the way and as you become a better player you will be able to unlock them gradually. Sometimes you will even have to bend the rules of the game to be more successful. But remember to never break the rules of any strategic game. The outcome of a strategic game is determined by how well you plan and organize your resources. The key to winning is simply managing your resources. If you just leave yourself on autopilot mode, you'll never get very far.

A dreadfully disproportionate number of people around the world are playing this money-game without having the rudimentary knowledge about how the game is to be played to be successful. More than 90 percent of all the players are not even aware of the rules of the money-game. No wonder why there are so many losers out there. Even the highly educated and highly paid professionals often fail when it comes to this money-game. This is because the subject of money and personal finance is not taught in schools. Even MBAs from the most prestigious institutes often find themselves behind the curve in this money-game. The funny thing is that most people are not even aware of the existence of this money-game we are forced to play.

The movie 'Moneyball' starts with a quote which goes like this - **"It's unbelievable how much you don't know about the game you've been playing all your life."** This makes perfect sense when it comes to the money-game. See, we can afford not to play games like basketball, or baseball, or soccer, or golf. But the money-game is one game which we cannot avoid. Everyone is bound to play the money-game unless one is in some isolated islands in the middle of the Pacific

Ocean or living as a hermit in some caves in the Himalayas.

When playing the money-game your 'income' is like your trump card. It is more important than mere possession of assets or having high net worth. To play well your assets and net-worth must always be converted into some form of liquidity. Though there may be capital appreciation and an increase in the value of your assets over time, their true potential can only be realized when they are converted into incomes. As long as they are not converted into some types of income their capacity to help you attain your financial freedom is very limited.

Financial freedom is the ability to live off from the income of your personal resources. Your resources only have the potential for financial-freedom, but to actually achieve financial-freedom the mere possession of personal resources is not enough. They must be transformed into income-generating assets to help you attain your financial-freedom. Specifically, they must be converted into a stream of 'passive incomes'.

What Is Wealth?

My favorite definition of 'Wealth' is from Dr. Buckminster Fuller as his definition is in line with the attainment of financial freedom. He measured wealth not just in terms of money but in terms of money's relationship with time. He defined wealth as: **"A person's ability to survive X number of days forward."** In financial terms, this is the same as saying 'If you stop working today, and stop actively earning money, how many days or years could you survive?'

The objective of financial freedom is to free up your time using money. However, there are two different approaches to freeing your time with money. The first one is to consider money as something stagnant. This is how most people view their money - in terms of net-worth and assets. The other approach is to consider money as something which is flowing, like a stream of water.

Let Us Try to Understand These Two Approaches Using a Suitable Illustration

Let's say you have an amount of US $100,000 and your monthly expenses are US $5,000. Then your wealth, according to Dr. Fuller, is US $100,000 divided by US $5,000 per month, which is equal to 20 months. Thus, if you have $100,000 in your possession right now you will be able to live for 20 months without having to do any work. In a way, we can also say that you have freed up 20 months of your time by having US $100,000 in your possession. So, let's say if you want to live freely for 50 years (or 600 months) on a US $5,000 a month expenditure you will be needing about US $3,000,000.

Let us take another example to understand money as a flow concept. Let us assume that you are in a job and earning active income. Over time you managed to save and invest a portion of your active income. Let's say your investment is now generating US $1,000 as passive income. Since your monthly expenses are US $5,000 you will be able to free up 1 month of your time for every 5 months of passive incomes through your investment.

Now, if you keep increasing your investment corpus you will eventually reach a point where you will generate US $5,000 per month as passive-income through your investment alone. An amount of US $750,000 giving returns of 8% per annum will generate this US $5,000 per month. Once your monthly passive-income equals your monthly expenses you are, literally, financially free. According to the wealth definition, this is the point at which your wealth becomes infinite i.e. you don't have to work another day. This is the point of your financial freedom.

From the above illustration, we can see that when you view money as something stagnant the amount of money required to buy your freedom is much more as compared to when you consider it as something flowing. This is where the power of income comes into play. So, if you know how the money-game is played you don't need a huge amount of money to be financially-free. You just need to understand the terrain to ensure that you make the best decisions with your money. Always know the rules of the game and try to make the best decisions with your money.

This is also the difference between being 'rich' and being 'wealthy', though most people use it interchangeably as if they are the same thing. Riches are measured in terms of money alone whereas wealth is measured both in terms of time and money. Your true wealth is your time and your freedom. Money is just a tool to help you free up your time. However, it is a powerful tool in the sense that it has the power to free your time. Sadly, most people focus only on getting rich rather than becoming wealthy. Remember the old saying **"Money talks, but true wealth whispers"**. If you are only superficially rich you won't have a sense of security and will try to impress others by showing offs. However, when you are wealthy you have a sense of security and will engage yourself in other things that don't involve the discussions of money or how much you have of it. It will speak quietly for itself.

Different Types of Income

Why do you need to know the different types of income? To be really successful in the money-game you must be very thorough with the different types of incomes as they are the main tools for helping you achieve your financial-freedom. It is only when you can specifically differentiate the different types of incomes and understand their natures that you will start to play well and can play to win.

Every endeavor in life requires certain knowledge, skills, and abilities that are essential for success. For instance, the Inuits have more than 200 different ways of describing the snow. This may seem strange, but snow is such a big part of their life that they need to describe the many different types of frozen water which is critical for their very survival. As they are permanently living in frozen places, many things that are related to snow are a matter of life and death for them. They must know the distinction between the snows that one can sink in from the snows that can be used for constructing their igloos, to the snows that are navigable from the snows that are dangerous. They have to know their depths, densities, and other different properties. Their very chances of survival depend on their being in harmony with the snow. They cannot survive without that knowledge.

Imagine if you are suddenly being forced to live in these permanently snow-covered landscapes, it will be challenging for you to survive and thrive. Unless you are willing to learn about the snow you will always be in potential danger. However, you must also remember that knowledge is only potential power. You have to act on the knowledge to make it powerful. It is only when you have gained enough knowledge and experience in the different types of snow that you will start having the confidence to go out and explore opportunities.

Similarly, the Arabic language has over 100 words for the 'camel' which at one point had as many as 1,000 words. In the olden days, these animals made life in the desert possible, providing everything from transportation to clothes and even food and milk.

According to the proponents of the Linguistic Relativity Theory, the structure and lexicon of our language influence how we perceive and conceptualize the world around us, in a systematic way. They contend that the languages we speak and the objects around us are interrelated. Our languages are mostly shaped by the objects surrounding us. In the same manner, our world is also built upon the languages we speak. Technology has also brought words into our lives more than ever before. Words are no longer just something we speak, hear, read, or write. They have become what we create and how we interact with the world around us.

Thus, you can deliberately change your life by carefully choosing the words you use in your daily life. By changing the words, you consistently use you can change the way you think, the way you feel, and the way you behave. You can achieve your goals more quickly and bring your dreams to fruition simply by choosing the right words consistently. You can consciously use words to improve and change your life. So, choose your words wisely as it has the potential to shape your life.

How you speak to yourself also directly influences your outer world. If you develop the habit of positive self-talk, chances are that your external world will also turn out to be more positive.

So, starting today you can begin changing your life by deliberately changing the words you use. You can start with one word and internalize it using repetition. Repetition is the most powerful tool to imprint something into your mind. It increases your mental validation of anything we are exposed to. Doing this can in turn shift your emotional patterns from negative to positive. Shifting your emotional patterns is the key to shaping your decisions, your actions, and your life.

We can also liken incomes to musical notes. To be a proficient music player you must first learn the musical-notes and how they combine to form chords and scales. Once you properly learn these fundamentals you can compose any number of songs and produce different musical harmonies. Similarly, when it comes to money and accumulating wealth you have to master the various types of incomes and combine them to strike some financial harmonies and chords and create multiple sources of income.

Coming back to the money-game, most people know income only as income and cannot make proper distinctions between the various types of incomes. This makes it difficult for them to effectively play the game. Different types of incomes can be used for different types of strategies, and sometimes leverage one's strategies to have an edge. The sooner we learn these subtle differences the better. You have to use a combination of different types of income to accelerate your journey to financial freedom. You need not make it too complicated, but you should at least be able to effectively combine them to your advantage. With this knowledge, you will have a better chance of succeeding in the game and coming out a winner.

So, let us delve into the various types of incomes, their significance, and how to use them to the best of our abilities. This will increase our chances of winning the money-game. Just knowing the different types of incomes will go a long way in playing the money-game effectively and will put you way ahead of the majority of other players.

The different types of incomes can be broadly divided into two categories: Active Incomes & Passive Incomes.

Active Incomes

These are the types of incomes that require your active involvement. When you are not engaged the incomes also stop coming. Doctors, lawyers, and other professionals earn active incomes through their practices. The moment they cannot perform their practices, for whatsoever reason, their income also stops.

One important precept of generating active income is to trade time with money. As you cannot multiply yourself nor your time this type of income is inherently limited, however big the income may be. It is also really not possible to leverage such income generation. Though it is also possible to attain financial-freedom through active-income sources, one needs to have a really big income for that. Only a handful of people have made it through the active-income route.

Some common examples of active incomes are income from a job, from professional services, from labor, from businesses, etc.

Initially, active incomes are a necessity as they are usually one of your first sources of income. However, you'll have to apply your mind, and creativity, to quickly convert your active-incomes into the more important source of income, passive-incomes.

Passive Incomes

Passive-incomes, on the other hand, are the incomes generated from the investments of your resources. It is money making money. It is your money working for you. Your resources, if properly invested, will generate incomes even when you are sleeping, working out, traveling, spending quality time with families, or doing whatever you like. The legendary stock market investor Warren Buffet once said, **"If you don't find a way to make money while you sleep, you will work until you die."**

However, you must also remember that initially, passive-incomes are not at all passive. You will have to put up a lot of hard work and effort. You will also need patience and perseverance. Initially, you will not be able to generate large amounts of passive-incomes. Building a portfolio of passive-incomes also takes time. You have to have a focused and unwavering mindset directed constantly towards your financial goals. Any deviation must be monitored constantly, and course corrections must also be made all along the way. But, I promise, you will be grateful to yourself for having gone down this road. In the end, it is worth the effort. It is like trekking to a beautiful place. The climb may be difficult, but the view and the happiness you derive upon reaching your destination is worth the effort. When it comes to the money-game your reward is financial-freedom.

Presuming that you are not inheriting a huge sum of money or winning a lottery and that you are not a very rich person, the first place for you to start building your passive-income stream is to convert your active-incomes into passive-incomes. This means you will need to allocate a portion of your active-income for that purpose only, which we will call a financial-freedom fund.

Your goal is to reach your financial freedom point as soon as possible. Your financial-freedom point is the point where the income from your resources and investments exceeds your expenses. The moment your passive-income exceeds the daily expenses you no longer need to work for money. Even without working, you will still have excess money to further grow your financial-freedom fund. As your passive-income grows you can also enhance your lifestyle and buy more toys. But the cardinal rule is to always stay within your means, that is not to spend more than your passive-income.

The different types of passive-incomes may include interest incomes, dividend incomes, rental incomes, residual incomes from royalties, etc.

The Income Gap

This is the most important gap of all the gaps. Even if you get only this one right you are set for life. It can be written as 'income minus expenses' equals 'savings and investments.

INCOME - EXPENSE = SAVINGS & INVESTMENT

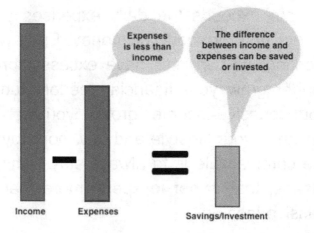

This is also the basic tenet of all teachings on personal finance and financial literacy. Here you are required to save a certain fixed percentage of all the money that passes your hand as income, both active-incomes as well as passive-incomes. No amount is too small or too large. It is not really about the amount of money. It is more about the habit. As we are creatures of habits the sooner you develop this habit the better. You can start with any amount. You can start with a dollar. But whatever percentage you have decided to save-and-invest, you MUST do it. As long as you can keep this gap in the positive i.e. expenses are lesser than the income, your financial life will also be in the positive. You will be swimming with the flow, not against it.

This is a simple formula which is easy to do. But the reality is that most people could not even meet their daily expenses from their active income alone. What is easy to do is also often easy not to do. Their income-expense equation is like this:

EXPENSES - INCOME = DEBTS & LIABILITIES

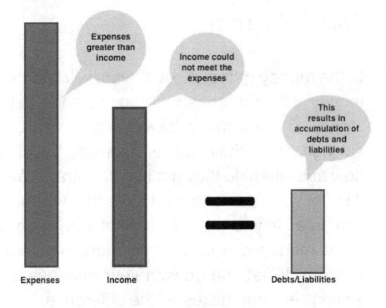

When expenses exceed the income most people will bridge this gap with borrowings and credit card debts. They are in the negative zone, swimming against the tide. Initially, the debt may be a small amount. However, if one is not careful this debt can easily snowball into a bigger amount, which will then have the negative impact of compounding interest. This is how people got themselves trapped in this vicious debt-cycle for the rest of their lives and become a slave of their creations.

How People Got Themselves into This Debt-Trap

In the money-game, most players will find their money inflow increases throughout the initial stages. They usually have surplus cash, or savings, from their active incomes. But then how and when do they get into debt-trap? Well, it is not what you earn and save that will make you free. If you are not careful with money, more money can only invite more problems, not less. What you do with your earnings and savings is what makes all the difference.

People tend to associate money with anything that will give them instant gratifications (more of this will be discussed in the chapter 'The

Creativity Gap'). So rather than investing the money, they end up buying toys that they don't need. But the story doesn't end there. Most toys need some cash to operate and maintain them. Also, people do mental accounting of any surplus cash available from their active-incomes and start borrowing money for their homes and cars. They are balanced so far. However, a slight increment in expenditures, due to unforeseen events like a car breakdown or medical emergencies will easily render the equation into a tailspin. They will then try to close this gap using credit-cards and expect to pay off the outstanding amount the next month. But comes next month and they end up paying only the minimum due and carry forward the balance amount to the next month. So, with all the maintenance charges on their toys, mortgages on their loans, and the interests on their credit-card borrowings the small gap rapidly widens and becomes a financial quicksand in no time.

There are different schools of thought on the issue of using debt. And there is no one right or wrong method. It all depends on the person who uses it. As for me, I don't like debt as I consider it to be a dragging force. I prefer swimming with the flow, not against it. I want to always be positive with the gap. However, sometimes debt is good if it has the potential to return more money in the future than the cost of borrowing it. It also has the power of leverage if properly deployed. So, one very important rule of the money-game is to not borrow money, except for things that can earn you back more money. Just don't borrow money for consumptive purposes. Credit cards can best be avoided as they are purely meant for consumptive buying.

Another important point to note here is to always live within your means. This is a low-stress strategy for keeping the income-gap positive. However small your income may be as long as your expenses don't exceed your income you will be in the positive zone. And through proper investment of this surplus cash, you can further widen the gap, which in turn will bring in more cash. If done consistently over some time, this initially small gap can easily grow in size through the power of compounding interest. A point will soon come when your income from your investment corpus will exceed the income from your active engagement. This is the point of your financial freedom.

Strategies to Maximize This Gap

There are two different ways to increase your income-gap. Remember that initially, all your incomes might be active-incomes, but eventually, you must convert all your active-incomes into passive-incomes. It is only with passive-incomes that you will attain your financial freedom. Remember true wealth is created, not earned.

Defensive Strategy

This strategy assumes that the income is fixed. So, you have to tinker with your expenses. Your goal is to cut your expenses as much as possible to increase the income-gap. Identify all the holes in your pocket, big or small, and plug them as soon as possible. You can do this by meticulously tracking where all your money goes. Then you group them into categories like groceries, medical bills, electrical bills, telephone charges, internet charges, entertainments, etc. Once you have done this exercise you will begin to see a pattern. Then you put aside all the essential expenses where you cannot make any reductions. What you need is what you need. But you will also definitely find out that there are many non-essential expenses which can be easily managed, and some which can be eliminated. People can easily reduce somewhere between 25-30% of their expenses by using this method. And your investment corpus will grow to that extent, which through compounding interest will take you much faster to reach your financial-freedom goal.

The Offensive Strategy

In this strategy, you put all your focus on the income side of the equation and do nothing with the expenses. You endeavor to increase the income-expense gap only by increasing your income. You can do this by taking up a second job, or through side hustles, or investments. This additional income will directly add to your 'savings and investment' side of the equation, which in turn can further be deployed for generating more income.

Of the two strategies mentioned, I prefer the offensive strategy. However, both strategies have their pros and cons. The defensive strategy requires a lot of discipline on your part and you may have to compromise on some of the fun that you love doing. The offensive strategy on the other hand often becomes stressful, especially when you take up a job just for the sake of increasing your income, and not because you love the job.

What I advocate is that you use the combination of both the strategies for a set period, say 2-3 years. You should think of this period as an investment of time and sacrifice everything for the sake of your financial freedom. The gap generated during this period will greatly accelerate your journey towards your financial freedom. Even a small incremental gap will make a huge difference once you factor in compound interest over a long period.

Chapter 5: The Time Gap

The Time Value

Time is one of the most precious possessions we have as it is in limited supply. Anything of limited supply is valuable. We all have only 24 hours a day. If you want to spend your time well, you have to know the difference between a wasteful way of spending it and a productive way of spending it. A productive way of spending time is to invest it for your future self. The reason why most people waste time is because they can't make a distinction between the two. You must also not waste time doing something that you don't like or enjoy. You must treasure your time and always make the best use of it and not waste it.

As time is finite you must always have a detailed plan on how to properly utilize it. Although time is of limited supply most people don't realize its value and spend their whole life wasting it for doing something they don't like.

Most people trade their time for money, which is the worst form of tradeoffs under the sun. It is true that initially, you might have to do something that you might not like and trade your time for money, but make sure that it is a temporary ordeal. It is your duty and your birthright to escape this time-money tradeoff at the earliest. You must set targets to free yourself from the clutches of this trade-off. You must diligently do whatever necessary to free yourself within a given timeframe.

To successfully set goals and free yourself from the time-money tradeoff you must have a thorough understanding of how the time-money tradeoff operates. And to know this you must be able to dissect and analyze the time available at your disposal.

Time, being intangible, is best understood using suitable illustrations. Let us assume that you are 30 years old and that your life expectancy is 80. To visualize this you draw a straight line and break it up into 80 equal parts.

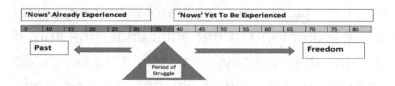

Your past is already gone. There is hardly anything you can do to change this portion. However, your future is the time that is yet to be experienced. You can express your future in different units of time - 50 years; 600 months; 2,607 weeks; 18,250 days or even 438,000 hours. When you express time only in terms of years it becomes obscure and we often get carried away and our mind goes into automatic mode saying there is still plenty of time left. However, when you express your time in terms of months, or weeks, or days or even hours you will start seeing and realizing how limited your time really is. This is because we can better relate with the smaller units of time as we know how quickly an hour or a week or a month passes us by. You see how limiting it sounds when you say that you have only 600 months to live, or 2,607 weeks to live or only 18,250 days to live.

Now, once you know how limited your time really is would you still want to waste another day, another week, or another month? You have to think twice to do that.

Now let's go back to the diagram once more. You are now in your 30th year. Whatever had happened in your past has actually brought you to the point, who you are and what you have become today. At the present it is also pertinent that you should ask some retrospective questions like 'Am I happy with who I have become?', or 'What could I have done better in my past that would have drastically changed who I am now today?'.

It is found that most people felt that they could have done much better given a second chance. However, as we all know that our time is limited, and what is already gone could never be brought back to the present. There is no point in focusing too much of our attention in the past. It will be just a waste of energy. It is gone. It's best to forget about it.

However, we will direct our entire focus in the future, your 30-80 years. You should again ask some hard questions about your future - 'How would I like to spend the time available in the future?', 'What are the things that I would love to do in the future?' 'What type of a person will I become in the future?'

Once you are clear about all the choices and things that you want to accomplish in your future it is time to put our focus back to the present.

The Time Gap

The time-gap requires that you must put all your focus, your attention and your energy to achieving your financial-freedom within a limited period of just 3-5 years, and thereby freeing yourself for the remaining 45-47 years. That is all it takes to free yourself.

However, you must do whatever it takes during these 260 weeks or 60 months. You must endure and be resilient. If needed you have to trade your time for money during this short period. You must learn to delay your gratification. You must not waste an hour, or a week, or a month. Every waking moment should be channelized towards the achievement of your financial-freedom goal. The payoff at the end of the day will bring much greater satisfaction.

Once the future is freed from the clutches of the time-money tradeoff you can do whatever you want with this time. You can travel the world, you can write books, you can spend quality time with your family or do some community charity works which you have been planning to do. No one can stop you from doing what you love to do. There will be no more bosses, no more waking up to the alarm clocks, and no more rushing through the traffic. The irony is that people tend to make more money doing what they love because they can produce more value. More value equals more money because value attracts money. That's how our reality works. This is the time-gap which you must strive to achieve.

During this struggling phase, you must do whatever it takes to attain your financial freedom. You must save not less than 50% of whatever you earn during this period. You can even cut down on your famous lattes during this period. You can cancel all your unnecessary subscriptions and channelize all the savings to your financial-freedom fund. You can forget all the expensive habits like smoking, drinking alcohol, etc. Don't even take a vacation during this period. No eating outside, no expensive clothes, and no expensive toys. Period. This is the period when you really work for your financial-freedom fund. This is the period when you really build up your army of money-soldiers who in turn will bring in dividends and interests in the future.

This is the period for you to write books, create videos, websites, or even start-up businesses. I am one hardcore advocate of the view that there should be a very large sacrifice made during these early years.

I know you might be thinking that this is too much, and it will be difficult. But I can assure you that if you stick to your plan the payoffs will justify your struggle. This is an offer which you must not resist. It is a question of your freedom. The tradeoff - 260 weeks of hard work for 2,346 weeks of freedom is much more sensible than 5 days of hard work for 2 days of freedom, for the rest of your working life. Working hard for just 60 months and freeing up 540 months is a much better choice than working for the rest of your life and living paycheck to paycheck.

Back from The Future Thinking

To achieve this time-gap sometimes it is best to visualize yourself into the future, say 10 years from now, and look back at your life from there. Think of exactly the kind of person you want to become 10 years from now. Assume that you are already there. Now from there, you think back all the way to the present moment. Ask yourself what are all the things that you would have done, starting today, that would ultimately take you there. These are the things that your future self would really be proud of.

Once you have identified all the things that you need to do to become the kind of person that you envisioned to become 10 years from now, you must put in all your energy and you focus and strive to accomplish them in just 3-5 years. And if you can accomplish what you envisioned yourself to do in 10 years, within a shorter period of say 3-5 years, then you can actually accomplish much more in 10 years through the compounding of your results. Whatever we do today will have a compounding effect in the future.

Time Perception

We often have the feeling that as we grow older time also passes faster, as compared to when we were younger. This is just a distortion in time perception, somewhat like an optical illusion. The fact is that we all have 24 hours a day - rich or poor, young or old, black or white, male or female, healthy or unhealthy, happy or unhappy, successful or unsuccessful.

Let me explain how the time distortion really happens. Our perception of time changes in direct proportion to the time we have already spent during our lifetime. Consider a child who has just turned 5 years old. Asking that child to wait for 1 year will be like asking him to wait for another 20% of his lifetime. However, asking a 40-year-old guy to wait for the same 1 year would be like asking him to wait for 2.5% of his lifetime. Hence this same amount of time will be perceived as relatively shorter by the 40-

year-old guy, as compared to the 5-year-old child. So, when a 40-year-old guy asks a 5-year-old child to wait for 1 hour before he can get his favorite chocolate, it will be equivalent to asking the same 40-year-old guy to wait for 8 hours before he can have his favorite beer. This understanding of time perception will also go a long way in understanding the psyche of a child, thereby making you a better parent.

There are different studies done on why this distortion in our time perception happens. Some say that it is because of the gradual slowing down of our metabolic process, which in turn slows down our biological rhythm. This gradual slowing down of our biological rhythm has a psychological impact on us and renders the world to be moving at a faster pace as we grow older, even if it were not. Some even attribute this phenomenon to Albert Einstein's famous Theory of Relativity and its time dilation. However, the Theory of Relativity is not just about the perception, but it measures the actual time distortion. Whatever may be the fact of the matter, what is important is that you must be aware of the existence of this distortion in time-perception and take advantage of it, rather than become a victim of it.

As we grow older, and if we are not careful enough, we tend to waste a lot of time due to this perceptive time-distortion. Even 3-5 years will seem a very short period and will be gone in no time. The intention is to make this time-distortion work in your favor. It can be used to leverage your journey towards your financial freedom. Struggling for 3-5 years will seem like a really short period if you are older. This short period will anyways pass away just like that, so why not utilize it to free yourself for the rest of your life.

The Only Time We Have Is 'Now'

Strictly speaking, there is no past and no future as far as time is concerned. Everything happens in the present, in the 'here and now'. Let's simply call what we currently experience as the 'Now'. What we call our past is actually a collection of 'Nows' that had already occurred. And what we call the future is also a set of 'Nows' which we are yet to experience. We can only live in the 'Now'. In fact, it is claimed that the Hopi people of Arizona have no words for time and therefore could not conceive of time as a linear flow of past, present, and future. They basically exist in the 'Now' as we know it. In fact, they don't even have a word for 'Now' because to step back and call it something would take them out of the 'Now' itself. They just exist at the moment.

What we really experience in life and what really matters is what we do in the 'Now'. We must maximize our experience in the 'Now'. That is all that really matters in life. If you want to be happy in life, spend more time gaining experiences and less time accumulating stuff. Things can always be replenished with more things. Money can also be replenished with more money. But our time, our 'Now', is limited. The time-gap is to trade some of your 'Nows' which you will experience earlier in life for freeing up most of your 'Nows' that will happen in the latter part of your life. If you don't sacrifice some of your earlier 'Nows' for better 'Nows' to be experienced later on you will end up experiencing very lousy 'Nows' for the rest of your life.

If you are not careful you can end up trading most of your precious 'Nows' for money even after you have already accumulated enough money to free up all of your unused 'Nows'. This is what happened to most people. When you really do the math, you will find out that you don't really need a huge amount of money to free up all of your 'Nows'. You will also realize that the amount of money needed to maximize your 'Nows' to your wildest dream is much lesser than what you actually had in your mind. And for those who are content with little that figure is much lesser. Most people really needed more money just for show-offs, or to impress other people they don't really care about. As stated earlier your main objective is to free yourself, not to get rich. Socrates once said, **"He is the richest who is content with the least, for content is the wealth of nature"**.

Most people spend their time as if it is of unlimited supply and save every penny of their money as if it is very limited. Time is limited, money is not. We all have the same amount of time and you can make the most use of it if you sleep less, or waste less. Even if you don't sleep at all you will still have a maximum of 24 waking hours. It is limited. You cannot really multiply your time. You can however maximize your output per unit of time using different methods. You can leverage the amount of work done per unit of time through various techniques of automation, delegation, or elimination. Automation is to time as compound interest is to money. You can only do so much in one life. So, the key to doing more is not working more hours but learning how to get more done with the time you've been given. Unimportant and repetitive but non-negligible works can best be outsourced to a third party. Wherever possible its best to eliminate some works altogether.

In terms of management theories, the Pareto Principle shows that 80% of your results come from how you spend just 20% of your time. So, focus on how you spend the 20% of your time that helps you grow the fastest and master it. The remaining 80% can be outsourced or eliminated altogether.

A Brief History of Time Management

Throughout the history of time management, from Frederick Winslow Taylor to Peter F Drucker, the objective of time management has always centered around efficiency and productivity.

The various processes and tools developed by these time-management gurus are the direct outcome of the Industrial Revolution and the assembly-line of factories. Unlike the agrarian society, the factory workers had to learn to live by the clock, and not the sun. The assembly-line requires its workers to synchronize their time to the seconds. Otherwise, it becomes a bottleneck. As a result of this, punctuality and productivity were of paramount importance and had become the overarching goal of time management.

Our schooling system, which was in itself an outcome of the Industrial Revolution, is also designed as a training ground for working in a factory. If you are a good performer in the schooling system you are a suitable candidate for working effectively in a factory. The grading systems in schools are also designed as the requirements of the factories.

Steven R. Covey, in his best-selling book 'The 7-Habits of Highly Effective People' introduced us to yet another time management matrix using 'Urgency' and 'Importance' of an assignment, and how to prioritize your time using these factors.

So, the various time management theories that are in vogue are really designed to make you an effective factory worker. Even the more recent and refined theories are designed to make you an effective leader only in a business setting.

These time management theories are not designed to help you gain your freedom. To gain your freedom you must learn not only to spend your time effectively and productively but also to invest your time.

How to Invest Your Time?

Strictly speaking, there is no time management. You can't really manage time. You can't make it go faster or slower. You can't make it move forward or backward, and you can't make up for a lost time. You can only invest time, spend time, or waste time.

To invest your time, you must learn how to utilize your time in doing significant things. You invest time by spending your time on things today that will give you more time tomorrow. Always ask yourself 'How can I spend my time today that will make tomorrow better?'. Spending your time effectively by doing what is urgent, or what is important - as proposed by most time-management gurus - might be a really good way of performing your jobs, but it's not a good way to invest it. Urgency is how soon what you do matters, and importance is how much what you do matters. To really invest the time you must learn to do what is significant. Significance is how long what you do matters.

The more significant things you can do early on in life the more time you will be able to free up in the later part of your life. There is an opportunity cost involved in doing insignificant work. In life what we intentionally avoid doing is as important as what we actually choose to do. One must also be strong enough to say 'NO' when needed. Every time you say 'YES' to insignificant things you are also simultaneously saying 'NO' to significant things. Choose wisely.

Some of the ways you can spend your time in a significant way are learning new skills, reading books on self-development, automation of routine works, training your subordinates, building systems, physical exercises, etc. On the other hand, some of the ways you can spend your time insignificantly are binge-watching TV series, watching movies, listening to music, reading fiction, playing videogames, chit-chatting with friends, browsing through social media, etc.

When you learn new skills, it will pay dividends as long as you live. For instance, learning the art of public speaking may take time and effort. But its importance is for life. You must always learn new skills. It is one of the most effective ways to invest your time.

Automation of routine jobs and building systems can significantly free up your time. To illustrate the significance of automation and building systems let me take you through a small metaphor. Let us say you live in a small village where there is no water supply. The only source of water is from a brook nearby. Every time you need water you have to carry water from the brook. What conventional time management teaches you is how to find the shortest path from your house to the brook so that you can save some time in reaching the brook. It will also teach you how to carry three or four buckets simultaneously so that you become a more efficient bucket carrier. It will also teach you how to design better buckets so that you can carry them with minimal effort. These are perfectly fine, and they will help you become more efficient and productive. But the problem is that the next time you need water you again have to go and collect water from the brook, however productive and efficient the method may be.

Now think of how to spend your time significantly in this situation. One way is to build a pipeline which flows all the way from the brook to your house. It will cost you money and time to set-up the system. However, once the system is complete you no longer have to spend your time collecting water from the brook. Even if the rate of flow is small it will keep pouring in more water while you eat, while you sleep, while you engage yourself in other productive activities. Here, by building a system that automates the process of supplying water, you end up freeing all of your time, and energy, required for carrying the water. Your time and energy are freed not only for a day, or a month but for years. This is what I called doing what is significant.

If you can differentiate what is significant and what is insignificant and always strive to do what is significant you are bound to prosper. You will become unstoppable within a short period. If you don't spend your time well it's the same as burning money. To spend time on significant things, you should develop a more conscious approach to your commitments.

Chapter 6: The Action Gap

The distance between you and your goal of financial freedom is not 'time' but 'actions'. Make that your brain tattoo. Time is variable but the number of actions is fixed. Most people set their goals only in terms of time. They say that they will become successful after some obscure period.

It is, no doubt, good to have a specific timeline for achieving a goal, but at the same time, it is also important to realize the fact that it is not the 'time' per se that determines your success. It is the number of actions that you put into within a given timeline that really determines whether or not you will achieve your goals. This is also one of the reasons why I always vouch for 'massive actions.

You might often come across people telling you 'Why work hard? Is it not better to work smart?' But always remember - 'working-smart' is not a substitute for 'working-hard'. You must work hard, even if you are not able to work smart. However, you should also try to work smart whenever possible. Working hard and smart at the same time is when the magic happens.

There are so many talented and smart individuals out there who are financially broke. On the other hand, there are also really dumb people who are obscenely rich. The one who works hard will always beat the smart guy if the smart guy doesn't work hard enough. In a way, this is also liberating. You don't always have to be smart to be successful.

Laws of Averages

According to the author and motivational speaker, Jim Rohn, if you do something often enough a ratio will appear. He calls this ratio the 'Law of Averages'.

According to this law if you talk to 10 persons and convince 1 person the ratio is 1:10. If another person talks to 10 persons and convinces 9 persons his ratio is 9:10. Once you know these ratios you can always beat the other guy by using this law, and by working hard. You can beat the guy who talks to 10 persons and convinces 9 persons by talking to

100 persons and convincing 10 persons. This is a fine example of a hard worker beating a smart guy.

Goals, Actions, And Timeline

When you set a goal for a specific timeline, say 10 years, it is implicit that you are required to put in a certain fixed number of actions during these 10 years to achieve your goal. Without actions, a goal is not a goal. It is merely a wish.

When setting a goal, you write down all the action plans for the entire timeline. Let's say you set a goal and plan to achieve that goal in 10 years. For simplicity sake let's say you intend to put in X number of actions, Y number of actions, and Z number of actions during the entire duration of 10 years to achieve your goal.

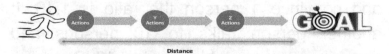

Now you can start seeing the distance between you and your goal in terms of actions. Once you know this distance between you and your goal it is really up to you to spread the action across any time horizon. The amount of time you need to achieve your goal is immaterial as long as you put in the required number of actions. What you need to achieve your goal is 'massive actions'. You no longer need to be smart or talented to reach your goal as long as you are willing to put in the required number of actions to reach that goal. This is what I call the Action-Gap.

In the action-gap, I suggest you curtail your timeline to about 30 percent of the actual timeline which you had set for yourself to achieve a goal. You can truncate a 10 years' timeline to 3 years. Most people feel that bringing down the timeline to 30 percent is not possible, or it will be too difficult. But the fact is that it is very much doable and possible. We have been, unknowingly, doing it all the time through the process called procrastination.

When we set a goal in terms of 'time' it is a human tendency to assume that there is always enough time to accomplish the goal. This in turn will delay the actions. It is only at the very last moment, just before the dateline, that people tend to really put in the actions and still somehow manage to complete the tasks or achieve the goals.

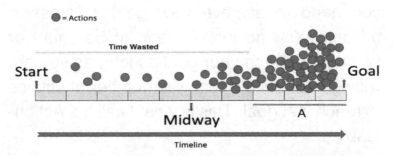

From the above illustration, it is clear that the number of actions is not evenly distributed during a given period to achieve a goal. Very few actions occur during the initial first half of the period. The actions started gaining momentum only past halfway through the timeline. It started piling up only towards the dateline. The period A is the zone of maximum actions. Here, the zone before A is basically time wasted because as long as you don't reach your goal your mind will not be free to engage in any other worthwhile pursuits.

With the action-gap the objective is to intentionally shift this action-zone towards the beginning and complete the entire actions within 30 percent of the timeline.

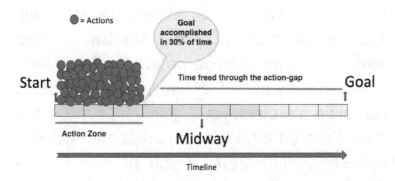

30 percent can be considered the goldilocks zone. If you are overambitious and try to bring it down to about 10 percent or 20 percent, you will increase your chances of burnout. On the other hand, if you increase it beyond 30 percent you will end up wasting a lot of time. However, once you have brought down the timeline to about 30 percent you have to work hard, and smart if possible. You have to put in massive actions. There is no substitute for hard work if you want to be successful.

Action-Gap and Management Concepts

The action-gap concept is also in tandem with some of the most common management concepts in the management world. Consider

Parkinson's Law, which states, **"A task will swell in proportion to the amount of time you give yourself to complete it."** Essentially if you give yourself a long enough time to complete a project, you'll give it less focus and it will drag on for a longer period than actually necessary. Therefore, if you have a shorter deadline, you'll produce a much higher-quality output in a more focused period.

Vilfredo Pareto had also stated that 20 percent of your time will result in 80 percent of the desired outcome. It is this 20 percent of your time that we will focus on completing 80 percent of your goal. Another additional 10 percent of your time will be used to complete the rest 20 percent of your goal. Now you see how doable that 30 percent is. It is how you trick your mind to intentionally achieve 100 percent of your goal in just 30 percent of your allotted time. This is some clever stuff.

Action-Gap and Focus

Another good reason for bringing down your timeline to 30 percent is that it will help you in staying focused. You will also be required to focus all your attention on the pursuit of your goal. There is tremendous power in focus. A set of actions spread across 10 years will be much less effective as compared to the actions focused within a much lesser period of, say 3 years. The simplest analogy is harnessing the power of sunlight through a magnifying glass.

It is only when the sunlight is condensed into a much smaller area, through the use of magnifying glass, that it will become effective. It will now be able to burn holes in papers and fabrics. Putting a matchstick under the sun from dusk till dawn will not ignite it. However, if the same matchstick is put under the focused sunlight of the magnifying glass it will ignite in seconds. Now, you can save the entire day to do something worthwhile instead of the futile wait for the matchstick to ignite. That is the power of focus. That is the power of the action-gap.

Devoting your limited time, attention, and energy to achieving a small number of important goals will dramatically increase your chances of success. Isolating the important ones from the less-important and less-urgent ones is half the battle. Also, in life, anything that you put your focus on will grow. Life without focus is simply a blur. Always decide on what to focus on and what not to focus on. That will make a whole lot of difference in the quality of your life.

"The road to happiness lies in two simple principles: find what interests you and you can do well and put your whole soul into it - every bit of energy and ambition and natural ability you have."
—John D. Rockefeller

It is also true that in life you will not always be in a position to decide the datelines. For instance, if you are pursuing a course with a specific timeline you have to stick to the timeline. There is nothing you can do about it. However, we are concerned with what you have control of. You have total control over what timeline you set for achieving some of your personal goals. We are talking about only what is in your zone of control. Whenever you have control, reduce the timeline to about 30 percent of the actual timeline and put in all your energy and efforts in that 30 percent time.

Chapter 7: The Creativity Gap

God has created us in His very own image and likeness. Hence, we are God-like beings endowed with immense creative powers. We are designed to be creators of our realities and destinies. We all have the power to be the scripters of our own lives. We were never really created to be victims of our circumstances.

Until not very long-ago man derives his happiness purely out of his creative pursuits. He is a producer. He builds things out of his tools and plants crops and harvests them. He paints, composes songs, music and does all sorts of creative activities though for his pleasure. The intention was never to sell his creative products to make money. That comes much later. He was contended in his world and hardly makes any comparisons with others whatsoever.

Unfortunately, due to a lack of proper understanding and awareness of our God gifted creative potentials we've unknowingly ended up creating a life we don't desire. With the advent of the Industrial Revolution and its consequent assembly-line mass-production economy, the world was flooded with all sorts of products. Then comes the advertisement industries who were pushing these products to every nook and corners of the world. Today we are being bombarded with thousands of messages about one product or another daily. Competition amongst different industries also instills in us a sense of comparison. We started comparing the things that we have with our neighbors and our near and dear ones.

Our happiness and contentment started drifting away from what is inside of us to what is outside. That is the point where we started losing control of our attitude and behavior itself. We started buying and hoarding things even beyond our requirements and means. We buy things on credit. And we started deriving a false sense of happiness in the process. We have become victims of these thought patterns and habits. We end up becoming mass consumers.

As we become more and more consumption-oriented our self-worth, our self-esteem, and even our meanings in life have become more and more obscure. As we can't derive true meaning in the consumption of things, we no longer have a true purpose in our lives. On a larger scale, it is also this excessive consumption-oriented mindset that has led to all sorts of ecological imbalances and pollution in the world. It has also led to the creation of a huge wealth gap. According to study, the world's richest 1% own half the world's wealth. The top 10% of the global population holds 85% of the world's total wealth, while the bottom 90% hold the remaining 15% only.

To understand how we have become so hooked onto the consumptive process let us try to figure out what drives us towards this kind of behavior. To do that we have to look into the biological aspects of our behavior, especially how some of our hormones shape and consolidate some of our acquired behaviors. A proper understanding of the same will go a long way in shaping our behaviors to our advantage.

The Role of Dopamine in Shaping Our Behaviors

Dopamine is a neurotransmitter that is responsible for sending signals to our brain. It is a powerful chemical that is responsible for experiencing pleasure and making us want to do things. It is secreted naturally when certain activities are performed, and its release is satisfying and pleasurable. Its primary function is to motivate us to perform certain acts. It was originally developed to reward us and encourage us to engage in activities that will help us survive and will benefit us evolutionarily - eat when you are hungry, drink when you are thirsty, run when in danger, reproduce, win competitions, etc. All these are natural processes of releasing dopamine.

However, our brains have since gotten too smart for their own good. We have invented addictive-drugs to artificially stimulate our brains and do things recreationally instead of for our survival. We get pleasure from these activities because they stimulate the same areas of our brains as sex and food. For the same reason, our thoughts and behaviors too can become addictive. If left unchecked these thoughts and behaviors, which are automatic, may be pleasurable in the short term but can have devastating effects in the long run.

Brain Stimulation Reward

Brain Stimulation Reward was discovered in 1953 by James Old and Peter Milner at McGill University. Old and Milner showed that electrical stimulation of certain regions deep in the brain was so rewarding that rats would self-stimulate those regions to the point of collapsing from exhaustion and starvation. They contend that humans too if allowed to electrically stimulate the reward system, would self-stimulate themselves in the same manner. The brain regions triggered were part of the reward system which generates desires, motivation, and learning. Electrical stimulation triggered the release of dopamine just like food, sex, and addictive-drugs.

Even when the stimulation was accompanied by electric shocks the rats wanting the brain stimulation would endure electric shocks stronger than what a starving rat would endure getting food. The rats were paying a high price to get the brain stimulation. Human addicts will pay just as high a price for their rewards.

On the other hand, if you can somehow block the dopamine secretions the mice will no longer be motivated to do anything at all. Without the release of dopamine, you don't get the work and you don't get the behavior. Even when food is placed in front of them, and even if they are starving, they will not make any effort to eat the food. Only when the foods are placed in their mouths will they eat.

So, we can say that dopamine release is in itself not a bad thing as they are necessary for motivating us to perform certain actions. If properly harnessed, they are capable of eliciting goal-directed behaviors. But too much of it through artificial methods is not good as it defeats the very purpose of dopamine secretion. The focus here is shifted more towards the dopamine itself and not the behavior they intend to elicit. If left unchecked we can end up doing things only for the sake of releasing dopamine into our system, even if the actions for that are self-sabotaging.

Areas of The Brain

There are three main areas of the brain that are often associated with addiction - the prefrontal cortex, the limbic system, and the midbrain.

The prefrontal cortex is responsible for all the executive functions of the brain such as decision making, logic, and reasoning. This helps us to decide whether or not something is good or bad.

The limbic system is the reward circuit of the brain. This is responsible for remembering a lot of pleasant experiences and reminding us that perhaps we could do it again in the future.

The midbrain is responsible for all our survival functions - our hearing, our vision, or our flight-or-fight responses. The midbrain is concerned only with what we do in the next 15 seconds. It does not view anything past that amount of time.

When addictive-drugs, alcohol, or psychoactive drugs are administered into the system it unleashes an inhuman amount of dopamine, something that you can never get from any natural experience. When that happens even the brain has a hard time figuring out how much dopamine is in the system. It then releases another neurotransmitter known as glutamate which is responsible for our memories. The glutamate acts as the glue that makes the synapses bond together thereby helping us in remembering the pleasurable experiences hardwired into the synapses in great detail. It is because of this detailed memory that the midbrain becomes more and more sensitive to the need of using drugs and alcohol. For a long time, we believed that our memory is to remember the past. It is actually to predict the future. This idea behind predicting the future is how motivational systems work.

The reason why drugs are so dangerous is that they short-circuit the survival pathways and hijack the entire dopamine system. Instead of gently stimulating it they slam it with chemical blasts far greater than that of any natural processes. The brain sets its priorities in large part based on how much dopamine it is going to get. As a result of this addictive-drugs and alcohol tend to be registered very high on the priority list of the brain as they can produce more dopamine than any other natural process.

Electrical stimulation of the brain triggers the release of dopamine much in the same way that addictive-drugs and natural reinforcers do. In a similar fashion social media feeds, pornography, gambling, videogames, etc. can also trigger the brain reward circuits, and hence they are also addictive.

If addictive-drugs and alcohol can be so dangerous to the nature of our brain that it completely rewires it into a repeated pattern of use, why can't we just stop using them? Why doesn't the prefrontal cortex make the executive decision that drugs, and alcohol are not good, and we should stop using them altogether?

This is because the midbrain is closer to the spinal cord and all the incoming electrical signals are first triggering the midbrain before the prefrontal cortex can make any executive decision. By the time the signals reach the prefrontal cortex the midbrain is already activated, and the limbic system is already going crazy thinking that the drugs and alcohol are a necessity of life. Also based on the memory of your earlier experience your subconscious is already wanting you to readminister the substances. So, in essence even before your prefrontal cortex has the chance to consider the choice of whether or not it wants to use the drugs and alcohol your brain has already made up its mind.

In one experiment to study the mechanism of dopamine secretion researchers trained a monkey to expect a reward. Here the monkey is given a squirt of juice when a green light flash. The researchers found that at first, the dopamine burst was when the monkey got the reward. However, eventually, the dopamine bursts occur even when the light simply switches on. It is like the brain saying that it is anticipating a reward when it sees the green light. When the same monkey is trained with another blue light which has a 50-50 chance of getting the reward the researchers observed that in addition to the dopamine burst that occurs when the blue-light turns on, there is also an increase in dopamine surge as it waits for the reward. The unpredictable nature of the rewards system is what keeps the dopamine level surging. This principle is being successfully used by many game developers and TV Serial producers to make their products addictive. Dopamine secretion is much higher with an anticipation of a reward than the actual attainment of the reward. No wonder why so many people are hooked on to their TVs and gaming consoles.

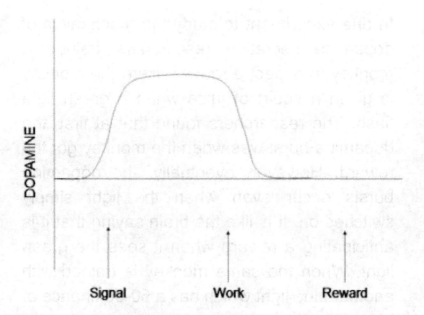

Video games are designed in this pattern of anticipation of rewards. People are addicted to video games, not because of the attainment of the rewards, but because of the anticipation of other rewards if you continue to play the game. And the cycle repeats itself.

Most of the social media feeds are also designed on the same principle. You are hooked to these apps and sites because you expect some 'likes' or 'feedback' to your posts. Or you are keen on knowing what others say or how they react to certain posts from someone you have known.

Most TV series are also designed on the same principle. One episode will end keeping you in suspense. This expectation and anticipation of what will happen next are what secretes the dopamine that keeps you hooked. You don't enjoy what happens when watching the next episode. But the next episode ends with another suspense to keep the dopamine flowing. This is the process of how people become hooked to these TV series without actually knowing why they are so hooked.

The same process can also be found in most of the best-selling books. For instance, look at one of the most popular books of all time, 'Think and Grow Rich' by Napoleon Hill. This book is no doubt one of the best books ever written in personal development and personal finance. However, it is not the content that keeps readers hooked on reading the book. Napoleon begins the book with a promise that you will find the secret hidden in his book as you read the book. He did not mention where or what exactly is the secret. He only mentions that there is a secret and that you will find it as you read the book. This is what keeps the readers hooked, the expectation to find the secret.

In today's world, the highly stimulating activities that we want to do are all over the places - shopping, social-medias, junk foods, pornographies, videogames. We are also constantly being bombarded by information all the time. The impact is that our dopamine system is being overstimulated and desensitized. This can hamper the quality of our life and our performance.

Mobile phones, social-media, videogames, etc. bring with it multiple, well documented significant harms. These devices are designed to fragment our attention as much as possible during our waking hours. They feed directly into our dopamine reward system and their tools are designed to be addictive. For instance, we have become so addicted to our phones that survey reveals 10 percent of people admit to checking their phones even during sex! There is a growing amount of research that shows that if you spend a large portion of your day in a state of fragmented attention it can permanently reduce your capacity for concentration. And if you lose your ability to sustain concentration, you are going to become less and less relevant to this economy.

Frequent video-game play is not inherently a problematic behavior - but when the play becomes compulsive and takes over other activities, or results in significant harm to major areas of functioning, you may owe it to yourself to make the distinction.

Dopamine is responsible for all sorts of addictions and habits. Most of the addictions are related to the consumption process. In consumption the dopamine release is instantaneous. However, in the creative process the dopamine released is delayed, but eventually more gratifying. People who are addicted to drugs and narcotics and alcohol are like those mice who will press the lever despite the electric shocks. The process of dopamine secretion is highly addictive especially when the activity results in the instantaneous secretion of high levels of dopamine.

Dopamine plays a huge role in shaping and modifying our behaviors. Dopamine is not responsible for the pleasure per se. It is responsible for the anticipation of pleasure. It is what pushes us into actions. It is about the pursuit of happiness rather than happiness itself.

We become consumption-oriented because this process of dopamine secretion is tied to our behaviors and habits. The advertising industries are well aware of this fact and made them work in their favor to maximize their profits.

Like the Pavlovian dog, we are also in a way conditioned to secrete, not saliva, but dopamine at the sights of commercials. This process of dopamine secretion on consumption-oriented activities results in all sorts of addictions. People may not be necessarily addicted to drugs and alcohol, but most people are addicted to their smart-phones, social media, video games, TVs Series, fast-foods, shopping so on and so forth.

This is not to say that all types of dopamine secretion are bad. On the contrary, the non-secretion of dopamine is bad. As seen in our mice experiment when the dopamine secretion is stopped, we will no longer be motivated to perform any tasks, take actions, create things, or produce things.

Dopamine Detox

Dopamine detox is the idea that you intentionally set aside some time away from the highly stimulating activities and let your dopamine system recover. It is the process of starving yourself of all instantaneous dopamine secretions by removing all the dopamine-producing objects and activities. It could be your TV, your gaming consoles, your smartphones, your favorite food from your favorite restaurants, the internet, pornography, shopping, or advertisements of any forms. The aim here is to render yourself in such boredom that even the simplest and most boring task becomes enjoyable. To illustrate, let us imagine a plain bowl of rice. This might not be appealing as compared to your favorite food from your favorite restaurant. But after starving yourself for 24 hours and when you are really hungry you will devour that bowl of rice. The ultimate aim of dopamine detox is to channelize your dopamine secretion process to the various creative activities and not the consumptive activities.

In comparison to the consumptive process, the creative process of dopamine secretion takes more effort and discipline. The consumptive process of dopamine secretion is easy and hardly requires any effort. It is also instantaneous and results in immediate gratification. However, in the creative process, the dopamine secretion does not happen immediately. It occurs long after the actual process is over. This results in delayed gratification. The ability to delay gratification is also a hallmark of a truly successful person. This is the reason why one has to intentionally engage oneself in the creative process. Unlike the consumptive process, the creative process will not happen automatically. You have to set certain rituals and time to engage in the creative process and stick to that routine no matter what. Initially, it will be difficult. But given enough time you will start to gain momentum and the process can even be made automatic eventually. In any creative process, the most difficult part is getting started. Once started, though, getting ahead is just a matter of following a set routine.

Though gratification is delayed in the creative process the satisfaction derived from the creative process is much higher as compared to the immediate gratifications from the consumptive process.

So, what I am trying to drive home with you is that you must be aware of your sources of dopamine if you want to be happy and financially free. I am not advocating here that you should abstain from all forms of consumptive activities and indulge yourself only with the creative process of dopamine secretion. Far from it. That would be me asking you to do some impossible things as a human being. However, you must be able to differentiate between your sources of dopamine as a creative process as against the consumptive process. Once you can identify and differentiate between the two you should always strive to intentionally engage yourself in doing more of the creative process as compared to the consumptive process.

The gap here is to always engage yourself in more of the creative process as compared to that of the consumptive process. As long as you maintain this gap you are on the road to eternal abundance. You don't create values through the consumptive process. You create values only through the creative process. The greater the gap you can maintain the sooner you will reach your financial-freedom point.

A technique I have developed for myself is to intentionally engage myself in the creative process and use the consumptive process to reward myself once the creative process is done. This way I can ensure that I am always ahead in the creative process and maintain a positive gap. The consumptive process is also important as it provides the raw materials for the creative process. For example, after reading lots of books on a given topic you will end up having enough ideas to write a book of your own on the same topic. Or, after watching several YouTube videos you will end up with enough plots to create your own videos. The trick is whenever you are indulging yourself in any consumptive process always have the intention to ultimately create something of your own. This way you will always have enough ideas to create something on your own.

A Little Words on Creativity and Abundance

Thoughts become things. That is creativity in its simplest form. Whatever you see in the world around you is created at least twice. Once in the head and then in its physical forms. Vincent Van Gogh used to say, **"I dream about my paintings, and then I paint my dreams"**.

The easiest way to convert your thoughts into things is to put them in writings. That is usually the very first step in any creative process. It may not be the final product, but the final product is usually built upon the written down thoughts. All human progress follows a similar path. Think about all the human inventions and creations - houses, buildings, bridges, engines, airplanes, ships, cars, rockets, dams - they all exist first in the minds of the creators, which are then put on paper and replicated in its physical forms.

Any person who engages himself in the creative process is on the creative plane. Operating from the creative plane is like tapping directly into the infinite abundance of the universe. It is much more powerful as compared to operating from the competitive plane. In the competitive plane, you have to take someone down to alleviate yourself. Your potential success is also limited in the competitive plane. However, in the creative plane, you are your own competitor. Your potential success is also unlimited. In the competitive plane your success usually only benefits you, but in the creative plane, your success will benefit a large number of people.

The Healing Power of Creativity

Creativity, expressed in whatever form, can save us and guide us to our true selves. It adds vitality to our lives. Creative activity is one way of tapping into the vast potentials lying in our subconscious mind. Dreams also help us tap into that vast resource of our subconscious mind. However, we don't have control over our dreams. We cannot decide what to dream about. But we have total control of how to express ourselves creatively. Engaging ourselves in creative activities is the conscious method of tapping into our subconscious mind.

Creativity is also like a muscle. The more you use it the stronger it becomes. The creative process helps us in becoming who we really are. That in itself is the healing power of creativity. It has the potential to heal our inner wounds and improve the quality of our life. It even has the potential to physically heal us by helping us to reach our full potential. It has the potential to expand the scope of who we are and what we can really become. It helps us uncover our untapped talents, abilities, and ideas.

People often say, 'get out of your comfort zone'. But I think a bit of more relevant advice would be to say, 'expand your comfort zone'. The creative process helps you become more comfortable with the unknown and the unfamiliar. It helps you expand your comfort zone. People do not venture into the unknown not because they are comfortable where they are, but because they are familiar with where they are. They may not be comfortable but the very fact that they are familiar holds them back. People often prefer a familiar yet uncomfortable position rather than venturing into some unfamiliar, but more comfortable positions. It is the fear of the unfamiliar that is holding them back. This is the reason why people would continue with their uncomfortable 9-5 jobs even when they know that there are opportunities out there that can guarantee

them to leave their boring jobs for a higher
return and greater freedom.

Chapter 8: The Compounding Gap

Compound Interest is one of the most important concepts for wealth creation over a long period. It is when the interest you earned on your investments earns interest itself. It is what causes wealth to rapidly snowball. An understanding of the power of compound interest is also essential to change our entire perspective about money. Albert Einstein once said, **"Compound interest is the eighth wonder of the world. He who understands it earns it; he who doesn't, pays it."** You can make Compound Interest work for you or against you.

Warren Buffet made most of his wealth by harnessing the power of compound interest. He accumulates about 99 percent of his wealth after his 50th birthday through compounding interest alone. He has neither invented anything nor sold anything. His net worth in 2020 is around $73 billion. He once said that the three things that made him successful are: **"Living in America for the great**

opportunities, having good genes to live a long time and compound interest".

One of the reasons why we cannot naturally think in terms of compounding interests and thereby harness the power of compound interest is because we humans are hardwired to think linearly (more of this in the latter part of this chapter). Bill Gates had rightly said, **"Most people overestimate what they can do in one year and highly underestimate what they can do in ten years".** This is because our minds are conditioned to think only linearly, and we are not able to factor in the effect of compounding over a long period.

Another reason why most people could not harness the power of compound interest is simply that they don't do the math. Moreover, compound interest takes time to deliver its magic and most people are short-sighted. They also lack the patience to let the compound interest do its wonders. However, most of the wealth in the world is created, not by people working hard for money, but by money working for money through the power of compound interest.

When you work for money the amount of time you can trade for the money is limited. Hence the income from it is also limited. It increases linearly and there is a limit to how much you can earn since there is a limit to the number of productive hours that you can work. Even if you put in 20 hours of work a day your income is still limited as you can only do so much. When you work for money you are also literally selling your time for money. You are simply trading your most valuable possession with a limited amount of money. By the way, why would anyone set a limit to their earning potentials?

If you learn the art of multiplying money with money through the power of compound interest, there isn't any limit to the amount of money you can make. Initially, the process may be slow and the returns meager. However, given enough time it has the potential to generate returns beyond your wildest imaginations.

Another good thing about compound interest is that it is scalable. You can always enhance the process of wealth creation through compound interest by starting early, and by intentionally putting in more money at an early age, rather than waiting for a small amount of money to snowball into a huge amount. This scalability of compound interest is called the compounding gap.

There have been numerous illustrations cited in various books to show the importance and power of compound interest in the wealth creation process. Here also I will bring in a few such illustrations.

The Rice and Chessboard Story

There was a famous legend about the origin of chess in India. It goes like this. When the inventor of the game demonstrated it to the king, the king was so impressed with the invention that he decided to reward the inventor and asked the man to name his reward.

As a reward the inventor wished to be given one grain of rice for the first square of the chessboard, then double the number of grains for every subsequent square till all the 64 squares are covered.

The king and his ministers were amazed at the request and made a mockery of him for asking such a small reward - or so they thought. However, a wish is a wish, so the king granted him the wish and asked him to collect his bag of rice in a week.

Before the week was over the king was informed that they don't have enough rice to give to the man as per his wish. The rice would add up to an astronomical quantity, far greater than all the rice available in the whole world put together. We will not discuss what happened with the king and the inventor afterward.

I don't know about you. But looking at the chessboard and the condition of doubling the rice every subsequent square, my initial estimate of the reward could not go beyond one bag of rice. Even when I forcefully stretched my imaginations it's still difficult to go beyond ten bagsful of rice.

However, when I do the math what I found is mind-boggling. I still find it difficult to contain the actual quantity of rice that I've arrived at on the 64th square. I am simply not used to thinking about such a huge quantity. For illustrative purposes let me reproduce the calculations.

According to Google 1 grain of rice is 0.029 grams. So, if we calculate the weight of rice in kilograms it comes to a whopping more than 534 trillion kilograms of rice! The number of rice grains is more than 18 quintillion! I had to Google the term quintillion as I have never come across that figure earlier. By the way how long would it take to count 18 quintillion of rice? There are 31,536,000 seconds in a 365 days year. If you take 1 second to count every grain of rice you will need more than 584 billion years to count 18 quintillion of rice grains. So much from a small chessboard!

The calculation is given in the table below:

Chess Board Number	No of grains of rice	Weights in Kilograms
1	1	0.000029
2	2	0.000058
3	4	0.000116
-	-	-
-	-	-
-	-	-
30	536,870,912	15569.25645
31	1,073,741,824	31138.5129
32	2,147,483,648	62277.02579
-	-	-
-	-	-
-	-	-
62	2,305,843,009,213,690,000	66,869,447,267,197
63	4,611,686,018,427,390,000	133,738,894,534,394
64	9,223,372,036,854,780,000	267,477,789,068,789
TOTAL	18,446,744,073,709,600,000	534,955,578,137,577

534 trillion kilograms?! You know just a fleeting thought would not lead you to that figure, or somewhere close to that. But that is the fact. It is revealed only when you do the math. This is also one of the reasons why it is always important to calculate your figures: be it financial-goal setting or financial-freedom corpus amount, passive income calculations, etc. Once you know your figure it becomes much easier to reach those goals.

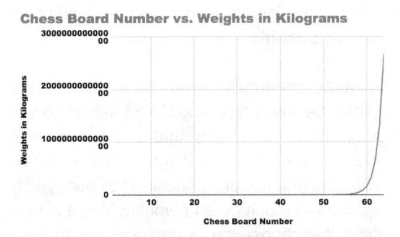

Chess Board Number vs. Weights in Kilograms

The author of the bestselling book **'A Random Walk Down Wall Street'**, Burton Malkiel, showed in one of his books the power of compounding through an illustration of two brothers, William and James, who invests money at 10 percent per annum for different periods. William invests $4,000 per year starting at age 20 and stopping at age 40. Meanwhile, James invests the same amount per year between the ages of 40 and 65. By the time William is 65, he has invested less money than his brother but has allowed it to compound for 25 years. As a result, when both brothers retire, William has 600% more money than James - a gap of US $2 million. This showed that one of the smartest financial choices we can make is to start saving as early as possible and harnessing the power of compounding as long as possible.

Another commonly used illustration is the choice between receiving US $3 million now or receiving 1 penny now that doubles in value every day for 31 days. If you do the math you will soon find out that choosing the penny way will lead to much greater wealth. Yet, it is very difficult to choose the penny gambit as the real payoffs happens only towards the end. The point I like to drive home here is that though a penny may seem a small amount, given sufficient time it can amount to a very huge sum of money through compounding interest.

Of course, the above two illustrations are extreme cases of compounding where the growth rate is taken as 100% for every chessboard or every other day. In the real world, such a high rate of compounding will not be possible in any kind of investment. The illustrations are just to show you how the compounding interest works, and how powerful it can be given enough time. The compounding period taken here is also very short, a unit of the chessboard, or in the second illustration a day. In the real world, the unit of time for measuring compounding interest is usually a year, and compounding interest is calculated considering many years to have its impact. The rate of compounding is also normally taken as 10% per annum.

To take reality into account let me take you through some real-life examples.

Benjamin Franklin and The Power of Compound Interest

Let us try to understand the power of compound interest through the foresight of one of the most influential founders of America - Benjamin Franklin.

At the time of his death in 1790, Benjamin Franklin was one of the wealthiest men in the United States. In his will, he had bequeathed 1,000 pounds sterling (roughly equivalent to the US $120,000 in 2020) each to the cities of Boston and Philadelphia, with an instruction that the money will be used to make small loans at 5% interest per annum. He had also instructed that much of the money would remain untouched for 100 years and the rest untouched for 200 years.

For simplicity's sake if we assume that the amount remains untouched for the entire 200 years the initial US $120,000 invested in 1790 at 5% interest per annum will amount to more than US $2 billion by 1990. However instead of at 5% interest per annum if the same amount of US $120,000 each were invested at 8.25% interest per annum (matching the US stock market's average return for the past 200 years) the ending value would have been a whopping more than the US $922 billion. That is the power of compounding interest over a long period. That is money making more money simply by sitting there.

The Purchase of The Entire Island of Manhattan for US $24

According to a letter written by the Dutch merchant Pieter Schage on November 5, 1626, to the directors of the West India Company, the European explorers had purchased the entire island of Manhattan from the Native Indians for a measly 60 Guilders worth of beads and trinkets.

In 1846 this figure of 60 guilders was converted to its then equivalent amount of US $24 by the New York historian John Romeyn Brodhead. This amount will be approximately equal to US $1,143 in 2020. So, the entire island of Manhattan was bought for the approximate US $1,143 only?

The answer is yes. And on the face of it, this deal seems to be the ultimate bargain. It is also often said that the Native Americans were taken for a ride and were looted by the European explorers. But were they? Let us do the math to find out.

If we assume that the Native Americans were able to invest the 60 guilders in some investment vehicle giving about 8% interest per annum that account will be able to buy back the entire island of Manhattan, in today's value, not once, not twice, but multiple times over.

This is the power of investing and compounding interest - money making money. Even if compound interest is the only thing you remembered from high school and you put it into practice, you'll still make it big in life. That is the magic of compounding!

It is pertinent to note here that in both the above cases no one is actively earning money and pumping back into the investment corpus. It is just the initial sum of money sitting still and reproducing through the power of compounding interest, over the given period.

The Compounding Gap

To harness the power of compounding interest most financial books will teach you to invest some initial amount of money and let the compounding interest do the magic over a long period of say 30-40 years. The truth of the matter is that very few people have the discipline and patience to wait for 30-40 years to get rich. Compound interest sounds good in theory but sometimes difficult to implement practically.

We have also seen that for any given amount invested over time the effect of compound interest will mostly happen towards the end of the period.

In the compounding-gap what we will try to do is to ride the power of compound interest early on in life by deliberately bridging the time. This will involve massive actions and sacrifice for 3-5 years. However, the dividend you will reap will far outweigh the sacrifice you have made. If you can harness the power of compound interest early you will be able to free yourself more quickly from the clutches of money.

Let us assume that you are 20 years old and that you have invested US $15,000 at 10% interest. This amount will become US $1,093,357 by the time you attain 65 years of age.

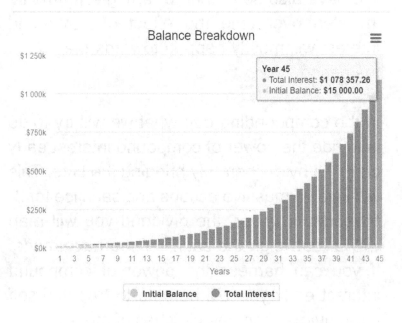

Balance Breakdown

Year 45
● Total Interest: **$1 078 357.26**
● Initial Balance: **$15 000.00**

Initial Balance   Total Interest

If you look at the graph you will observe that by the 35th year of your investment i.e. by the time you are 55 years old your investment corpus amounts to US $421,536.55. This is the same as saying an amount of US $421,536.55 invested for another 10 years at 10% interest amounts to US $1,093,357.

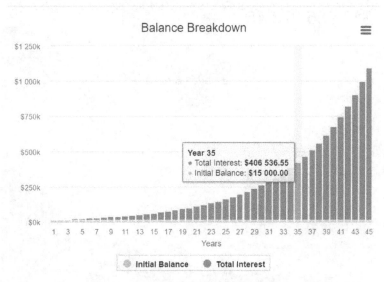

Balance Breakdown

Year 35
• Total Interest: $406 536.55
• Initial Balance: $15 000.00

Initial Balance   Total Interest

In the compounding-gap what we do is not to wait for the 35th year to arrive at the figure of US $421,536.55, but to arrive at this figure in another 3-5 years i.e. at least by the 5th year of investment, i.e. by the time you turn 25 years old. To be on the conservative side let's say that you could arrive at the figure by the time you turn 25 years old.

Now if you have US $421,536.55 by the 5th year of your investment, or when you turn 25 years, and stay invested till you turn 65 years, i.e. investing it for another 40 years, you will arrive at US $19,078,430.45 by the time you turn 65 years of age. That's a difference of US $17,985,073.45.

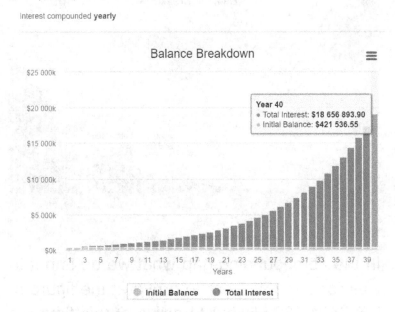

This will be the same as investing US $15,000 for 75 years at 10% interest.

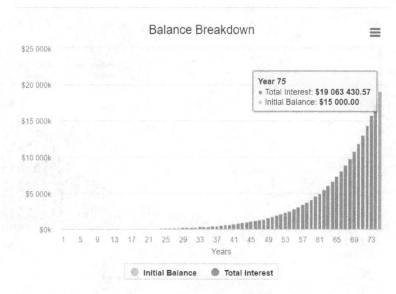

Balance Breakdown

Year 75
- Total Interest: **$19 063 430.57**
- Initial Balance: **$15 000.00**

Initial Balance   Total Interest

And if you are more ambitious and put in more effort and can accumulate US $1,000,000 by the time you reach 25 years of age, instead of the US $421,536.55, you will end up with US $45,259,255.57 by the time you are 65 (45 years of compounding).

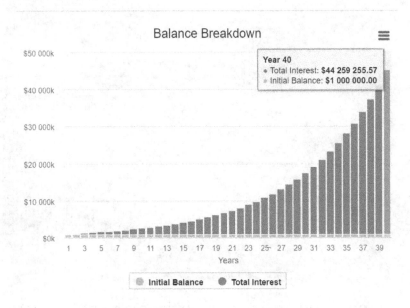

In any compound interest examples, you will observe that most of the growth happens towards the end. To harness the power of compounding interest it is always best to attack the graph towards the beginning, rather than just wait for the graph to explode towards the end. The trick is not to wait for the amount towards the end, but to try and reach that level of money sooner.

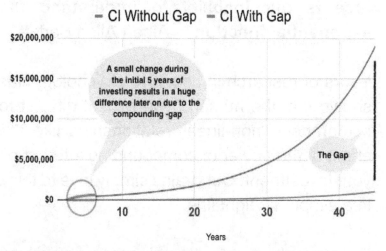

CI Without Gap and CI With Gap

The illustration above shows a comparison of investment of US $15,000 for 45 years with 10 percent interest per annum without the compounding-gap, versus another investment of the same US $15,000 for the same period of 45 years but with the compounding-gap during the initial 5 years.

"God, grant me the serenity to accept the things I cannot change, the courage to change the things I can, and the wisdom to know the difference" - Reinhold Niebuhr.

Linear and Nonlinear Thinking

"The greatest shortcomings of the human race is our inability to understand the exponential function" - Albert Allen Barlett

Years of research in cognitive psychology has shown that the human mind finds it difficult to comprehend non-linear relationships like the effect of the power of compounding interest on your investment. Our brains simply love to think in a simple straight line.

For example, a car with a higher fuel efficiency will always use less fuel than ones with a lower fuel efficiency. As such one should always go for the most fuel-efficient car. But the problem is that a similar linear increase in MPG does not result in a similar improvement in fuel savings. The more fuel inefficient a vehicle is, the bigger will be the improvement in fuel savings for a small improvement in efficiency. Replacing a car with a fuel efficiency of 10 MPG with one with a fuel efficiency of 15 MPG will save more fuel than replacing a car with a rate of 50 MPG with one with a rate of 55 MPG.

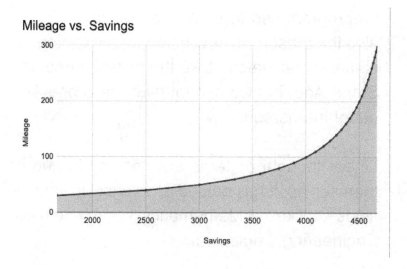

Mileage vs. Savings

Evolutionary psychology has also shown that our linear mindset was developed during our prehistoric past and it is hardwired into our brains. The kind of challenges we had during our prehistoric days when our brains were evolving, was mostly linear. As such our linear way of thinking had worked very well in those environments - predicting the movement of animals, tracking them and hunting them; or sensing dangers in our surroundings. Having a linear mindset was both reasonable and advantageous and had helped us to survive and thrive.

That is how evolution has preprogrammed our brains to think linearly. We are just not yet preprogrammed to think exponentially. This is also the reason why evolutionary psychologists contend that we can take the person out of the Stone-Age, but we cannot take the Stone-Age out of the person.

Linear thought patterns are not bad in and of themselves. It has helped us to excel in various fields like Mathematics, Accounting, Engineering, Logic, etc.

The problem with a linear mindset is when we overextend it to the nonlinear modern world. Human brains might be optimized for the world that existed 100,000 years ago, but they simply are not yet optimized for the modern world. Nonlinearity has become a fundamental part of the modern world, as the various technological developments are now growing exponentially and not linearly. All the technological advances that we surround ourselves with today haven't been around long enough for our brains to adapt naturally. Our brains are still the same as our prehistoric ancestors which made survival possible, and we are still relying on those traits today. We are still stuck with a mental module that finds it difficult to navigate through our current non-linear world. And this way of thinking has come in our way of truly comprehending and appreciating the non-linear relationships like the power of compounding interest. The worst part is that we are not even aware of it.

Linear thought patterns are easy to follow as we don't need to put in the extra effort. They are like weeds. They come automatically. A linear mindset is helpful in survival. No wonder why so many people are stuck in a job their whole life. This is because most jobs operate linearly and help us to survive. For the same reason, there are very fewer individuals who will embrace entrepreneurship, which is a nonlinear pattern, though the risk-rewards ratio is highly in favor of the latter.

How to Develop Nonlinear Thinking

To inculcate a nonlinear way of thinking we must first understand the way our mind works and its tendency to assume linearity. We must also develop greater awareness of the pitfalls of linear thinking in a nonlinear world. Awareness is the first step towards changing our thought patterns. Once you realize that your mind works linearly and that we live in a nonlinear world you must intentionally train your brain to think non-linearly daily.

Without proper practice, even experts, who are aware of the existence of non-linearity in their respective fields, often fail to take it into account the same and rely on their gut by default. Our intuitive system assumes that all the problems are linear. So, we have to consciously reboot and restructure our way of thinking to be able to think in a non-linear fashion.

Daily, you can pick one nonlinear function from the real world and analyze it. Try to understand how the various variables and the outcome are interrelated. If possible, try to make a visual representation of their relationships. Plotting in a graph will be very helpful. Seeing is believing. Once you make a visual representation you will start to grasp the implications. The visual representation will make it more real and easier to comprehend. Your calculations need not be exact. It is just to develop a nonlinear way of thinking - an exponential mindset.

You can work on the relationship between the speed of a car and its fuel consumption, the relationship between customer retention and profitability, the way the principal and interest portions got deducted in mortgage payments, etc. I, personally, like tinkering with compound interest apps. You can graphically see how different rates of interest and different periods affect the outcome.

Why Should We Learn to Think Non-Linearly?

Our way of thinking determines how we perceive the world around us, which in turn determines our actions and judgments.

"The world as we have created it is a process of our thinking. It cannot be changed without changing our thinking" - Albert Einstein.

Learning to think non-linearly will greatly increase our ability to make wise decisions. It will also help us to develop an exponential mindset which in turn will help us make better predictions.

Most problems in life are also non-linear. Life itself is non-linear. We set goals and expect to accomplish them in a straight line through time. But the reality is that the line between you and your goals is all squiggly. It will be riddled with failures and successes, highs, and lows. See, failures are just a part of the journey to achieve your goals. If you internalize this fact it will help you on your journey

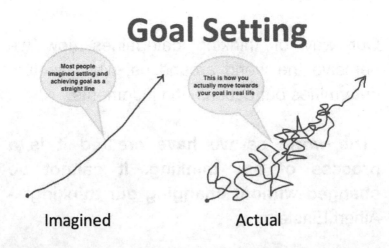

Goal Setting

Most people imagined setting and achieving goal as a straight line

This is how you actually move towards your goal in real life

Imagined   Actual

You cannot achieve your true potential if you do not teach yourself about the mechanics of your mind. In nonlinear thinking, we make connections among unrelated concepts or ideas. It will force you to tinker with your imaginations and help you come up with creative ways of solving complex problems.

The world we live in is evolving every day. It is up to us to make sure that our mind also evolves alongside it.

You should always strive to become a nonlinear, yet organized thinker. If you can do that you will be able to find connections between seemingly unrelated thoughts and then present it simply and clearly. This is critical for your success in many areas of your life. Become a disruptive leader and cultivate a culture of nonlinear, exponential thinking.

Chapter 9: The Investing Gap

What is Investing?

Investing is the art and science of allocating resources, such as time and money, intending to generate future benefits. It is about judiciously committing your time and money to improve your life and the lives of others.

Financially, investing is the process by which individuals commit their money to buy assets, such as stocks or bonds, to increase their value over time and to generate income in the future. It is a technique of building wealth for the future by setting aside some money today. It is making your money work for you and your future goals.

While the goals of investing may vary from one investor to another, the overall objective of investing money is to let your money grow big enough to generate passive income and make you financially free.

Though the history of investing is as old as the human civilization itself, and investment vehicles can be as diverse, here we're typically referring to the modern investment structure of the stock market.

So, what exactly is a stock market?

Stock Market

Originally the stock market is a place where investors, both individuals and institutional, come together to buy and sell shares of publicly traded companies. Nowadays most of these exchanges exist as electronic platforms and the trading of shares is being done electronically.

The Amsterdam Stock Exchange is considered the oldest Stock Exchange in the world. It was established in 1602 by the Dutch East India Company. In the US the first stock market was set up with the opening of the New York Stock Exchange in 1792.

Today, most countries around the world have their stock markets, and the stock exchanges have become an integral part of any country's economy. It forms one of the most vital components of a free-market economy. It acts as a medium through which the savings and investments of individuals are channelized to help companies raise large pools of capital for their expansion. In the long term, it helps the country's economic growth.

As a child, I used to think that money grows out of a 'money plant'. I soon found out that money doesn't grow on a money plant or any other trees for that matter. As I grow older, I realized that though money doesn't grow on trees there are ways and means to let your money grow. More wealth is created in the world by letting money grow on its own than by money earned through active pursuits.

To me, the stock market is like a giant 'money-garden' where anyone can plant and grow their money. You don't necessarily need to have a green thumb to successfully grow your money here. All you have to do is plant your money and follow some well-established successful gardening techniques. However, remember to keep your gardening activities as simple as possible. The system is already in place and you can make full utilization of it. This money-garden is one of the greatest inventions of mankind as far as investing is concerned. It is not monopolized, and anyone is free to own a piece of this fertile garden. This is the one place where you can make your money grow on trees.

In this money-garden, there are different investment vehicles for you to choose to plant your money. The size of your investment corpus is the size of your money-garden. You can begin with a small amount initially and slowly build up your corpus. There is also no limit on how big you can grow your money-garden. The sky's the limit.

Every investment you make should be treated like a seed or sapling planted. So, you have to have a long-time horizon. You should not check now and then to see how much it has grown. Or, dig them out and plant another seed if it is not growing as you had expected. Don't do that. That is not how you grow your investment trees. Instead, you have to carefully analyze the type of seeds before planting it. However, once planted it's best to forget it and let it grow on its own. You have to have patience. Over time some of the trees might be destroyed and lost completely. But the others will produce fruits or have huge cash values. Given enough time the trees will grow bigger and bigger and more and more fruits can be harvested. These fruits are technically called dividends. Initially, the fruits may not be much, but eventually, the fruits harvested in one season alone can surpass the initial cost of all the trees combined. That is the power of compounding growth through the stock market. You have the option of selling the fruits or replanting the seeds to produce more trees and more fruits.

As the stock markets are like gardens you should plant only that money that you can forget for a long time. Time is of the essence here. Don't plant money which you will be needing shortly for any reason whatsoever.

You can also simplify your investing process by simply buying small pieces of the entire forest rather than setting up your garden with selective seeds and saplings. This can be done through the process of indexing (more about this later). These forests are self-sustaining, resilient, and durable. They can better absorb any type of shocks that occasionally befall the money-garden and still thrive. They have successfully endured the Great Depression, two World-Wars, the Dot-Com Bubble, the Subprime Crisis, Black Monday, Black Wednesday, several financial crises, and stock-market crashes.

Just like in any real garden the money-garden also has its inherent risks. However, the risk is present everywhere. There is a risk when you cross the roads or when you travel in a car, bus, train, boat, ship, airplane. There is a risk even when you are sound asleep. When you keep an actual garden there is a risk of it being hit by a hailstorm, animals rampaging it, or pests and insects destroying it. However, no farmers ever stop farming or planting his plants due to fear of such calamities. Rather he learns to mitigate those risks and maximize his returns. Most of the time he will be making good returns from his endeavor. Similarly, though with inherent risks, wealth can be created in the stock market through regularly investing for the long term in a systematic and disciplined way.

There are various methods for setting up your money-garden. You can go for individual stocks and build your garden. Or, you can buy the entire forest through indexing. You can also outsource the process through the actively managed funds and insurance companies. There are also other instruments like bonds and CDs which are not common with small investors. There are also derivatives products like futures and options, which again are unnecessarily making the investing process complicated. We can stick with the fundamentals and keep the investing process simple and still be successful.

Let me elaborate on some of these investment vehicles so that you can make an informed decision for setting up your money-garden.

Company Stocks

Stocks are shares of listed companies. If you buy shares of listed companies you become part-owner of those companies, proportionate to the number of shares bought. Technically you are a shareholder and are entitled to receiving a share of the company's profits. The management of the company may decide to share its profits with its shareholders through dividends. Or, it may decide to retain its profits for future expansion. Whatever it decides to do it is usually for the benefits of the shareholders. As a shareholder, you also have voting rights to make certain decisions for the company. On the other hand, as the owner of the company you are also bearing all the risks that should befall the company. In any unfortunate event, you will bear the brunt.

Mutual Funds

Mutual Funds is an industry where you can outsource the process of stock-picking and portfolio management to a third party, a Mutual Fund company. Here you don't have to worry about which stocks will perform well in the future, or how much money you should allocate to certain stocks or bonds. These are all done by the fund managers on your behalf. You are outsourcing the entire process of investing in the mutual fund company by paying them fees.

Insurance Policies

Some insurance policies are being falsely promoted as investment vehicles by linking a portion of their cash value to the stock market. However, investing in insurance policies is one of the worst forms of investment available out there. To have a detailed view on the same you can refer to the chapter 'The Insurance Gap'.

Index Investing

Index investing, or simply indexing, is the process of participating in the stock market through the purchase of investment vehicles such as Index Funds and Exchange Traded Funds (ETFs).

Both index funds and ETFs are passive investing strategies that involve investing in an underlying benchmark index. They typically mimic the index exactly by holding all the index's securities. They do not deviate from the benchmark index irrespective of the market conditions. Both are considered to be conservative, long-term investment strategies. Both these funds allow portfolio diversification at low costs thereby maximizing returns. Indexing provides investors the opportunity to invest indirectly in an entire market without having to invest in the stock of the individual companies that it includes.

Though index funds and ETFs are mostly considered similar they have some subtle differences as well. They invest in similar portfolio shares but using two different methods. Index funds are mutual funds which are only priced at the end of the day, whereas ETFs are directly traded on the stock market like common stocks. Investors can also buy ETFs in smaller sizes and with fewer hurdles than index funds.

All said and done passive investments are not designed to outperform the market or a particular benchmark index. They are designed to help average investors own a piece of the entire stock market even with a small amount of money and have a truly diversified portfolio by simply mimicking the indexes.

The Investment Gap

The investment gap is to simply invest your money in the stock market through the process of indexing. Period. To support my claim read the following quotes from the legendary stock market investor Warren Buffett, **"The goal of the nonprofessional should not be to pick winners—neither he nor his "helpers" can do that—but should rather be to own a cross-section of businesses that in the aggregate are bound to do well. A low-cost S&P 500 index fund will achieve this goal."**

Though the thought of investing in the stock market scares many people, as it carries some element of risk, you must invest in the stock market if you want to achieve your financial freedom through investing.

Why the stock market? Because studies have shown that over long periods the stock market has been the best investment vehicle, generating returns far greater than those from any other asset class. And the smartest way to participate in the stock market is through indexing.

Why indexing? Again, because research has shown that about 92% of all the active fund managers fail to beat the index, such as the S&P 500, over any sustained long period. And out of the about 8% or so active fund managers that do beat the index, none of them can do it consistently. Most active fund managers consistently underperform the indices for more than five years. A ten-year winning streak against the index is almost unheard of in the investing world. Also, because index funds are much more easily managed than their active fund counterparts, their fees are also typically lower. And lower fees mean investors get to keep more investable money in their accounts.

There is indeed a possibility to outperform the index with actively managed funds, and this notion of outperforming the index may be very appealing to most investors. However, there is hardly any evidence to suggest that actively managed funds can consistently outperform the index. Though there may be some good active managers who can occasionally outperform the index, finding such managers in advance is all the more difficult.

As it is difficult to outperform the market indices, even by professional stock pickers, you are much better off simply putting your money in index investing. By indexing, you have a better chance of generating better returns as compared to investing through actively managed mutual funds.

Also, rather than buying individual stocks and attempting to create your portfolio you can achieve better returns by doing nothing and simply indexing. There are thousands and thousands of stocks out there, and it takes time and energy to properly research and analyze these stocks to make a proper selection. Thus, indexing can free up most of your precious time and energy which can be utilized for more precious things in life. You can use it for doing more productive work. You can also use your time to generate more income elsewhere which in turn can be used to buy more index funds or ETFs. This will greatly accelerate your journey towards your financial goals. You don't have to waste your time doing futile research and analysis to seek stocks in the hope that it will outperform the index. The chances of that happening are very slim to none.

Actively participating in the market is not worth the effort. Instead, by indexing, you can worry about other things while your investment corpus gradually increases in value. You can also avoid paying high fees to professional fund managers for picking stocks that are likely to eventually underperform the index. When you buy an actively managed fund you are handing over the job of picking stocks to the fund manager in the hope that he will beat the index and give you better returns. But will he? Many active fund managers try to beat the index by picking and choosing stocks, but they fail to do so year after year.

"When you look at the results on an after-fee, after-tax basis, over reasonably long periods of time, there's almost no chance that you end up beating the index fund." - David Swensen

Another problem with actively managed funds is that they are laden with fees. Some of the common fees are the expense-ratios, entry-load, exit-load, and Annual Maintenance Charges (AMCs). However, apart from these visible fees, there are normally about 17-20 different types of hidden fees. You have to have a PhD in Mutual Funds to know all these fees.

You might think that these fees are not large, but factor in time and compounding interest, and they will have a huge impact on your investment corpus. Your fees have a direct impact on what your investment returns will be. Fees are also one of the reasons why actively managed funds underperform their index and will continue to underperform the index. Even a 1% lead on an annual basis makes it increasingly difficult for active fund managers to beat index funds over long periods.

In one of the PBS documentary series Frontline Jack C. Bogle, the pioneer of index funds compared the performance of two hypothetical portfolios - one earning 7% returns without fees and the other earning 7% returns with 2%

annual fees. This 2% fee may not seem like much in any given year. But, assuming a 50-year investment horizon, the second portfolio would have lost 63% of its potential returns to fees, Mr. Bogle said.

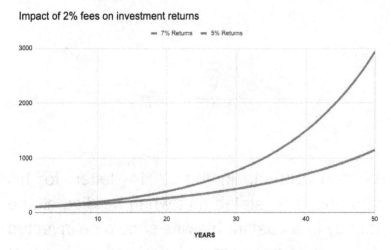

Impact of 2% fees on investment returns

━ 7% Returns ━ 5% Returns

YEARS

The longer the time horizon the bigger will be the impact of the 2% fees. If invested for 60 years, the 2% fees would have eaten 69% of the returns. In 100 years the 2% fees would have eaten 85% of the returns and so on.

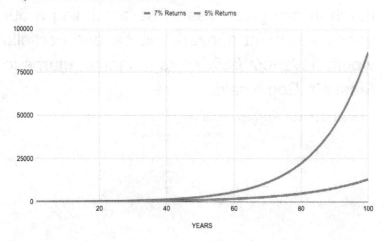

Impact of 2% fees on investment returns

— 7% Returns — 5% Returns

Warren Buffett, in his 2014 letter to his shareholders, stated that when he dies all the money in a trust for his wife should be invested only in indexes so that she minimizes her cost and maximizes her returns. He is so confident of professional stock pickers underperforming the index that in January of 2008 he issued a $1 million challenge to the hedge fund industry to beat the S&P 500 index over ten years. Protégé Partners LLC accepted the challenge, and the two parties placed a million-dollar bet. On December 31, 2017, Protégé Partners LLC conceded defeat ahead of the contest's scheduled wrap-up time. They were underperforming the index by a huge margin by then. Buffett contended that factoring in the fees, administrative costs, and other expenses, an S&P 500 index fund would outperform a hand-picked portfolio of hedge funds over 10 years. Evidence from a Barclays Global Investors study also shows that the chance is slim for an active manager to continue beating the index.

Always remember that investing and wealth-creation are long term endeavors. Don't ever look at investing as a way to make quick money. There are no shortcuts for growing wealth. To be successful in investing you must learn to stick with your long-term investment strategy regardless of the market movements. You'll reap the greatest harvests by consistently investing over time. The most successful investors are those who invest for the long haul. Small gains compounded over time with reasonable risk is how you build wealth.

Also, to be a successful investor you don't need genius level intelligence. A smart investor is one who can harness his or her emotions. The right temperament, and not high intelligence, is the key to successful investing. If high intelligence alone were the key to successful investing, top business school professors and economists around the world would be the wealthiest people on earth. On the contrary high intelligence can often be a hindrance to successful investing. This is because highly intelligent people have a hard time admitting even when they know they are wrong. They tend to think of themselves as always right. They are adamant about their decisions and continue to stick to their guns even when the market tells them otherwise. The great scientist Sir Isaac Newton himself became a victim of his intelligence when he speculated and lost about $3 million (in today's value) during the "South Sea Bubble" of 1720. Warren Buffett once said, **"Success in investing doesn't correlate with I.Q. Once you have ordinary intelligence, what you need is the temperament to control the urges that get other people into trouble in investing."**

Another important investing strategy is to start sooner and stay invested longer. Even if you only have a small amount, to begin with, it will be worth it. Initially, the amount is not important. It will gain momentum eventually. What is important is getting started and inculcating the habit. If you haven't started investing yet, you should consider starting right now. Remember the Chinese proverb which says, **"The best time to plant a tree was 20 years ago. The second-best time is now."** The power of time and compounding interest has the potential to work for itself for as long as you stay invested.

Lastly, good investing begins by investing in yourself and your financial education. Though it requires a little time and effort, financial education is one of the best investments you can make. It is a little effort now in exchange for a lifetime of financial freedom. The cost is little, the risk is almost nil, and the returns are huge. Financial literacy is the essential skill you must develop if your goal is to accumulate wealth and enjoy your financial freedom. There's no alternative.

Chapter 10: The Insurance Gap

What Is Insurance?

Insurance is primarily a tool for managing and mitigating risks. It acts as a safety net against any unforeseen future risks. Generally speaking, insurance is a system in which many individuals pool together funds and compensate for the losses that any of them may incur. This principle of spreading risks amongst many has been in existence since time immemorial. However, an individual can also self-insure oneself by putting aside enough funds to meet any future losses.

In common parlance, insurance is a form of a contract offered by an insurance company. An insurance company is a commercial entity which also acts as a financial intermediary. The contract is called an insurance policy. Individuals insure themselves by purchasing such policies and paying a fee, known as premiums, which is normally calculated as a monthly payment amount.

Though there are many kinds of insurance policies, some of which are required by law, we are mainly concerned with 'life-insurance' as it forms a very important component in your journey towards your financial-freedom.

Life Insurance

In life-insurance, the insured person pays monthly premiums to the insurance company for subscribing to a policy, and the insurance company is obligated to pay a specified assured sum of money to the family of the policyholder in the event of his death.

Why Is Life Insurance Important?

Life is uncertain and has a very uncanny way of throwing surprises at us when we least expect it. Also, risk is an unavoidable factor in the life of any individual. To be fully prepared to deal with such contingencies, life-insurance is very essential.

Life-insurance is important mainly because for so long as you are not financially free you will have people who are dependent on you and your income. As far as this book is concerned the main requirement of life-insurance is to replace your income in the eventuality of your death. This way your family can continue to get a guaranteed monthly income and maintain their lifestyle. Though nothing will be able to replace you, with the right kind of life insurance you have the assurance that your loved ones need not go through the additional burden of financial instability and hardships. It also has one very important intangible benefit - peace of mind. No amount of money can replace your peace of mind. Just the thought of knowing that your loved ones are protected, in case anything happens to you, will save you many sleepless nights.

With life-insurance in place, you can also take calculated risks and pursue your dreams without too much worry. With life-insurance you are financially prepared, come what may.

However, once you attain your financial-freedom, or stash out enough cash for emergencies, life-insurance is no longer a requirement. You are already self-insured when that happens.

Types of Life Insurances

Broadly speaking there are two different types of life-insurances: term-life-insurance, and permanent-life-insurance.

Term-life-insurance is the simplest form of life-insurance. It has low premiums and simple death benefits. It does not have any investment, or cash value component. It is only worth anything if you die and while the policy is still active. Yet it is the most effective form of life-insurance, as it provides the highest premium to coverage ratio. It is also very straightforward and easy to understand. As the name indicates, term-life-insurance provides protection only for a specified term, or period. However, once that period is over you can always renew the policy, or buy a new policy, in case you need more coverage.

Permanent-life-insurance, on the other hand, provides coverage that lasts the entire life of the policyholder, as long as the premiums are paid. It comes in many different varieties: whole-life-insurance, universal-life-insurance, variable-life-insurance, equity-indexed-life-insurance, etc. just to name a few. It generally has two components - the insurance portion and the cash value portion. The cash value component is a savings component that can be used as an investment account that builds value over time on a tax-deferred basis. The cash value is the amount that is available if you surrender a policy before you die, or after the policy reaches maturity. Because of this cash value component, permanent-life-insurance also costs more as compared to term-life-insurance.

One of the stated benefits of any permanent-life-insurance is that you get a guaranteed minimum return. Another frequently stated advantage of permanent-life-insurance is that you can borrow against your stashed cash value for various expenses such as down payments on homes and college tuition fees. Some policies even pay dividends.

The Insurance Gap

A little knowledge of the subtle differences between the two types of life-insurance policies will go a long way in your overall financial well-being. The insurance gap is to know the difference between term-life-insurance and permanent-life-insurance and buy only term-life-insurance, and that too only for coverage before you attain your financial-freedom. Doing that will greatly accelerate your journey towards your financial freedom.

Whenever you buy or consider buying life-insurance policies always remember to think of it in terms of buying an umbrella. There are different varieties of umbrellas. Though many people buy umbrellas for the color, the sizes, or the quality of materials, you want to buy umbrellas for its very basic purpose of protecting you from rain and sunlight. Most of the fancy umbrellas, with their designs and colors, are also unnecessarily costly. And when it comes to the function of protecting you from rain and sunshine, they are not very effective.

However, those umbrellas which are plain and simple, and which come mostly in plain colors, are the most efficient when it comes to the function of protecting you from rain and sunshine. So, when you buy an umbrella it is best to buy a plain vanilla umbrella and use it only when needed to protect you from rain and sunlight. They are simple, easy to operate, and efficient.

Like the umbrella analogy above life-insurances also come in different shapes and sizes. Just remember that whenever you decide to purchase any insurance policies there are professional salespeople who are making their living off of your choices in the process. Insurance agents and brokers are part of a business system that wants to generate as many profits as possible. They always try to collect more premiums than they shell out in claims. Naturally, most of the insurance policies that are being sold actively are the ones that generate most commissions to the insurance agents. They are not necessarily the best suited for you. It is truly said, **"You don't buy insurance policies, you are being sold one"**.

When compared with permanent-life-insurance, term-life-insurance is a much better choice. Some of the reasons why term-life-insurance is far better than permanent-life-insurance can be summarized as below.

Coverage: Enough coverage is very critical when it comes to purchasing life-insurance. If you don't have enough coverage with your life-insurance the very purpose of buying life-insurance policies, in the first place, is defeated. Too much of it is equally bad as too little of it. With term-life-insurance, you can easily buy enough coverage as the premiums are very low. However, with permanent-life-insurance, it is difficult to buy enough coverage as the premiums are way too high. This could also be one of the reasons why many people around the world are underinsured, without them knowing about it. Even if you know it, getting enough coverage with permanent-life-insurance can also place an unnecessary strain on your financial conditions.

Costs: Term-life-insurance policies are much cheaper as compared to permanent-life-insurance policies. Most permanent-life-insurance policies will be around 10-20 times costlier than the term-life-insurance policies. Permanent-life-insurances are also riddled with many hidden charges which are directly eating away the investment portion. Commissions on permanent-life-insurance can be as much as 80%-100% of the first-year premium. Then it gradually decreases over the years. This is how commissions slow down the accumulation of the cash value component of permanent-life-insurance policies, especially in the first few years of the policy. Overall 15% to 25% of all the premiums you pay over the life of the policy would go to commissions, fees, and other administrative charges. Permanent-life-insurance is one of the most expensive investments available out there. According to Jack Bogle, the founder of Index Funds, **"In investing you get what you don't pay for"**. This means that every dollar saved in fees and commissions will end up giving huge returns over a long period through the power of compounding interest.

In permanent-life-insurance the return on the investment portion of the policy is uncertain. It is not easy to figure out what part of the premium goes to pay life-insurance and what part builds up the cash value. The insurance companies are also not required to disclose this break-up. As such, it is not possible to calculate, or even presume any sort of 'rate of return'.

One funny thing about permanent-life-insurance is that you are paying higher premiums mainly for the cash value element of the policy. However, if the policyholder dies the beneficiaries will get only the death benefit portion. The cash value portion of the policy simply goes back to the insurance company! Why would anyone want to invest in something where you lose all your money if you die? Are people investing in permanent-life-insurance for the company or their heirs? That's a good question to ponder upon.

Simplicity: Term-life-insurance policies are straightforward and are the easiest to understand of all life-insurances. Here you decide the coverage amount and the period for coverage. Premium will be calculated based on these two factors and you pay the premiums. In case of death, your nominee will get the sum assured. When the term is over the policy simply lapses. However, you can renew, or buy a new policy, if you still need one.

Most permanent-life-insurance documents, on the other hand, are riddled with technical terms and jargon which only some professionals can unravel. Many agents and brokers themselves don't even understand these jargons. The premiums and fees are calculated by actuaries based upon some perceived risks and probability of certain events occurring in the future. As such only actuaries can understand how they work. It is not easily comprehensible for any layman. There are also many places in the permanent-life-insurance contract where an insurance company can make adjustments in the premium, the sum assured, etc. even after the policy is purchased.

Flexibility: When you buy term-life-insurance and invest the difference on your own you have the flexibility to withdraw the cash from your corpus in case of any financial emergencies.

And financial emergencies do happen. It's not a question of whether or not it will happen. It is a question of when it will happen. If you are in permanent-life-insurance and due to some unforeseen financial hardships, you are not able to pay the premiums the insurance companies will use the cash value of your policy to pay the premiums. The moment you run out of cash in your corpus and are not able to pay the premium, your policy simply lapses, and the coverage also ends. Thus, a slight change in financial situation could render you to lose all the progress that you have made through the years.

Duration: As stated earlier the main purpose of life-insurance coverage is to replace your income in case of death so that your dependents will continue to be provided for. If you plan to be financially free in 5 years, then you need life-insurance for 5 years. If you plan to be financially free in 10 years you need life insurance for 10 years and so on. Once you reach your financial-freedom there should not be any further need for life-insurance as it will be an unnecessary drain on your financial reserves when you no longer need protection.

With term-life-insurance, you can decide on how many years you want to get covered and pay premiums accordingly. However, permanent-life-insurances are for life. You have to pay premiums as long as you are alive. Otherwise your policy lapses. Theoretically, you can also encash the cash value portion of your insurance at any time. The very definition of cash value is the amount of money you would receive by surrendering the policy. But then the moment you surrender your cash value it practically becomes a surrender value, which is the cash value minus the surrender fees and various other deductions. Thus, surrendering a cash value comes at a heavy price as the surrender fee itself is around 10-15% of the cash value which greatly reduces surrender value. The surrender value that you get is also taxable. When you surrender you are also relinquishing the death benefit, which means your family will receive nothing from the policy when you die.

Diversification: When it comes to investment portfolios it is much easier to get proper diversification by buying term-life-insurance policies and investing the difference on your own. Even if you are not that savvy with the investments world you can go for indexing with very low costs (more on this in the chapter 'The Investment Gap'). Indexing provides enough diversification which is self-adjusted in line with the stocks that constitute the index.

When you buy permanent-life-insurance you are buying into an undiversified investment. You're investing a significant amount of your money with a single company. You are also relying on both the investment skill and the goodwill of their fund managers to produce returns for you. Study shows that more than 92% of the actively managed funds available out there consistently underperform the market indices. So, you will be much better off by simply indexing. Factor in the commissions, fees, brokerage charges, and the effects of compounding interest over a long period then you will start getting the real picture.

Retirement plan: All of us wish to achieve financial freedom at some point in our life. We also tend to believe that savings are enough to be financially stable. But if you look at life from a practical perspective you will soon realize that savings alone are not enough to attain financial freedom. Insurance companies and their agents usually refer to life insurance as an investment and a source of income for retirement. This is the sales pitch which they usually deploy to convince people to buy permanent-life-insurance policies. But the truth of the matter is that the returns on investments in permanent-life-insurance are very low as most of the premiums are eaten by commissions and fees. It is also not possible to calculate in advance how much you can expect to generate as income from the cash value of the policy.

To generate enough income for your retirement you should save and invest as much money as possible in good investment vehicles. Rather than paying high premiums with little coverage you can go for higher coverage with low premiums with term-life-insurance and invest the difference aggressively. Also, in permanent-life-insurance, you do not have any control over how the cash value portion is invested. Why would you want to leave your investment to chance when you can have full control of it?

Investments: Life-insurance is typically not a good investment, and, in most cases, you'll be better off avoiding it as an investment vehicle. Term-life-insurance does not have any cash value and hence cannot be used for investment purposes. Only permanent-life-insurance can be used as an investment vehicle. However, you can always beat the return of a permanent-life-insurance by investing the difference of premiums through indexing. The guaranteed return on investment usually stated for permanent-life-insurance policies is around 4%. However, after factoring in all commissions and fees, that 4% guaranteed returns yield only about 0.3%. And this 0.3% return is only after waiting for a long period of 30-35 years. The actual return on the investment value of a permanent-life-insurance is negative most of the years due to high commissions and fees in the initial years. Most of your premiums will go for paying commissions and fees before they go into your investment corpus. It takes a long time just to break even. In any type of investment, the lower the cost of the investments the better the performance tends to get. Cost is the surest and most dependable way to predict how an investment vehicle will perform.

I am not really in for putting my money into an investment vehicle which is likely to give negative returns for a long time. There are many investment options available today that can easily outperform the permanent-life-insurance policies as investment vehicles. So if you're looking for a way to invest your money permanent-life-insurance is rarely an ideal investment vehicle. Even if you make only a 1% return per annum on your investment you will still be better off than investing it in a permanent-life-insurance policy.

Also, you may be able to take a loan against your cash value in permanent-life-insurance. However, this is like taking a loan against your own money and paying interest to the insurance company. Why would anyone pay interest for borrowing their own money? Is that a good deal? Well, not for me.

Since inception insurance has always been used purely for protection. It was never looked upon as an investment vehicle, nor as a savings instrument. It was only in the recent past that insurance got confused with investments and savings. This is primarily the result of insurance companies falsely marketing insurance policies as a mix of insurance and investments. Most insurance companies and their agents are concerned only with their commissions, and not the welfare of the policy buyers. And since their commissions are being paid as a percentage of the premiums, agents have the incentives to promote only those products with higher premiums. This is also the main reason why they recommend more expensive insurance policies over cheaper insurance policies to the detriment of policy buyers.

When you are financially free you no longer need coverage as you are already self-insured. You no longer have to depend on third-party insurers. Also, if you have enough financial resources to guarantee your dependents' wellbeing you don't need life insurance. Or, if you have enough savings or investments so that all of your primary expenses are covered from the income from these investments, you don't need life insurance.

But for most people who are still in need of life-insurance, you are best off sticking with term-life-insurance. It is best to not confuse insurance with investments or savings. Keep insurance as simple as possible. Don't leave that decision to chance or brokers and agents. When you mix your insurance and investments it results both in inadequate insurance coverage on the one hand, and lower returns on your investment corpus on the other hand. Doing this defeats the very purposes of proper coverage of life-insurance and earning respectable returns from your investments.

Insurance companies and their products themselves are not useless per se. The trick is to find out which ones are good and which ones are useless. While you want to ensure that you're adequately protected, there are a lot of insurance policies that are unnecessary for most people. Purchasing the wrong insurance - or spending too much on insurance - can do more harm than good. Also, in the world of financial advisory, the only people who advocate buying permanent-life-insurance policies are the ones who are selling those policies. They themselves don't buy it.

Buy term-life-insurance for a projected period until you plan to achieve your financial-freedom. Save and invest the difference in premiums that you get by buying term-life-insurance over permanent-life-insurance. This will accelerate your journey towards your financial freedom. Also, the peace of mind you obtained from buying term-life-insurance is really worth the money. It is also a smart move.

Chapter 11: The Retirement Gap

Retirement as we know today is the practice of ceasing to work, in whatever profession or job one maybe, when a person attains a certain age. The current system of retirement assumes that a person is useful only while he is working. This way of thinking about retirement is an outdated concept. Generally, it is assumed that you work in a 9-5 job for 35-40 years of your most precious years, save enough money in some Social Security schemes, and stop working at the age of 65 living off those savings. Retirement is wrongly being projected as a part of a linear model of learning, work, rest, and die. It simply assumes that retirement is a place to stop, not a place to grow. It is really like dying before you actually die.

Relying on Social Security schemes today would be like relying on a tape-record player, which you had purchased in your 20s or 30s, to play music. You can still play music, but it's simply outdated. You will have a hard time buying new tape cassettes. Also, almost all songs are already available online in digital format, and they are just a click away. They are also cheaper and of better quality. Why would you still rely on that old tape-record player today? You would not. But when it comes to Social Security schemes most people are still banking on this outdated system.

Then why are we made to think of retirement like this? Why is retirement tied only to a person's age? Why are we not expected to retire earlier? Or, why are we not expected to continue working after 65 even when we are still healthy and capable?

To understand the above questions let us briefly look into the history and origins of retirement and pension funds.

History of Retirement and Pensions

In the beginning, there was no retirement. A person would continue to work and contribute to society as long as he is capable of doing something.

Retirement, as we know today, was first introduced in 1883 by the then German Chancellor, Otto Von Bismark when he announced that anyone over 65 years old would be forced to retire and that he would pay a pension to them. Many countries follow suit.

In the US, retirement as a concept was mainly the outcome of the Industrial Revolution whereby the aging employees were found to be slowing down the assembly lines or were taking excessive sick leaves. They were also holding on to positions where the more productive and profitable men could have been engaged.

The Social Security Act of 1935 was enacted by Franklin D. Roosevelt as a system for supporting the older retired people by the younger working people. The life expectancy in the US at that time was only 62 years, and the social security benefits were supposed to commence only on the attainment of 65 years of age. Hence, not many people were expected to receive retirement benefits. The few who received them were also not expected to retire for long. Roosevelt himself didn't live long enough to receive the retirement benefits as he died at the age of 63.

Today, with all the breakthroughs in medical technology life expectancy has been increasing over the years. For over a century now we have been able to add an average of 0.3 years to our life expectancy every year.

Retirement as initially envisioned was logical. But today the rules of the game have changed - people are living much longer, accounting rules are different now, the world has become a global village, and market volatility is directly affecting retirement funds.

Statistics have shown that half of all Americans say they can't afford to save for retirement. One-third have next to nothing in their retirement savings.

With a rapidly aging population and the baby-boomers retiring at a record pace, there is a declining worker-to-beneficiary ratio. There are fewer and fewer people putting money into the Social Security system and more and more people taking money out. The Social Security

Administration, in its 2020 Annual Report, estimates that it will go bankrupt by 2035 if no significant changes are made to how the system is funded. However, that's still a long way to go, and Congress will surely make changes in the funding process. But that's not the point. The point is that we should not rely on a system where we do not have any control.

"It is not realistic to finance a 30-year retirement with 30 years of work. You can't expect to put 10% of your income and then finance a retirement that's just as long." - John Shovan, Stanford University Professor of Economics.

Retirement Is About Income, Not Age

Successful people think of retirement in a very different way. The best way to look at retirement is to think of it in terms of your income and not in terms of your age. If you think in terms of age Parkinson's Law will set in, which states that **"A task will swell in proportion to the amount of time you give**

yourself to complete it". So, if you think you should retire by 65 years of age, you'll never be able to retire before you turn 65 years.

However, if you think in terms of income you have a number to work on, not some arbitrary point in the future. Once you fix your retirement income number you can immediately start working towards that number. Remember the wealth definition given by Dr. Fuller in the chapter 'The Income Gap'. That is what you should strive for. You must make your passive-income greater than your daily expenses. That point of your financial freedom is your retirement point because once you have reached that point you do not have to work for a living anymore.

Even before you reached your financial freedom point you can easily retire from your job as long as you can make the same amount of money doing what you love.

As was already described in the 'Goal: Financial-Freedom' chapter you have to determine the exact amount of passive income that you need to retire, and also set the exact date for achieving that target. Once the amount and the date are fixed your subconscious mind will start doing the magic and drive you towards your goal.

I can guarantee you that once you have achieved your financial freedom you will end up creating more values. You will retire from working paycheck to paycheck, or trading your time for money, but you will continue doing meaningful work. In a way, you will continue to do productive work even beyond 65 years of age. Also, you will work not because you have to, but because you want to. This freedom to do whatever you want to and not having to work for money is what I called retirement. By pursuing something you are passionate about or doing something you love, you will end up making more money in the process. This is also one of the reasons why the rich are getting richer.

Getting rich is much easier when you are financially free. It becomes almost automatic. You can become rich beyond your wildest dreams in just a short span of 3-5 years if you keep most of the gaps mentioned in this book in the positive. Always remember that the gaps have a multiplicative effect. The more gaps you can keep positive the quicker you will attain your financial freedom.

Retirement Is A Mindset

According to the award-winning journalist Dan Buettner, who explored the lifestyle traits of five places in the world where people live the longest, Okinawans have the highest life expectancy. He states **"In America, we divide our adult life into two categories: Our work life and our retirement life. In Okinawa, there isn't even a word for retirement. Instead, there's simply 'ikigai', which essentially means 'the reason for which you wake up in the morning".**

Today more and more people are viewing retirement not merely in terms of quitting their full-time job at 65 years and then living a life of leisure. They started viewing retirement as a choice, a transition from doing something one is forced to do to doing something one loves to do. Research has shown that people who retire by choice are much happier as compared to people who are pushed to retirement. So, my simple advice is to never let others decide what your retirement age should be. You must decide what retirement meant to you and at what age you want to retire, or not retire at all. Everyone has a right or a choice to decide when to retire.

Neuroplasticity and Retirement

Neuroplasticity is the brain's ability to form new nerve cells or new neural connections. This was thought to be of a limited phenomenon, mostly restricted to the early years of life. However recent studies have found that neuroplasticity continues throughout life, even in advanced years. A strong relationship exists between what we do with our brains and how our brains age.

Our brains, like our muscles, need constant stimulation to stay in shape. Without new information to work with our brain tends to stick to routines. Routines are advantageous as they help us in getting things done more quickly and efficiently. But without new information, our brains are not able to create new connections between neurons, which in turn causes our neurons and neural connections to deteriorate. This decline in cognitive functioning often leaves people at a greater risk of developing mental problems like Alzheimer's Disease.

In one experiment, called the Nun Study, Dr. David A. Snowdon, an epidemiologist at the University of Kentucky, and his colleagues found that there is a strong relationship between what people do with their brain and Alzheimer's Disease.

In this experiment 687 nuns, all above the age of 75 years, were studied to find out the reasons for their remarkably long lives. These nuns were also known for the absence of debilitating dementia among them. Their findings unanimously attributed this phenomenon to their lifelong habits of staying cognitively active. These nuns were found to constantly engage themselves in cognitive activities like solving crossword puzzles, reading books, playing card games, debating on current issues, etc. The study also found that those nuns with higher college degrees, who regularly engaged themselves in teaching and other mentally challenging activities, on average lived longer than their less-educated counterparts. Another important observation made was that before joining the order each nun had written a brief autobiography. It was found that those nuns who expressed themselves with more positive emotions in their autobiographies lived significantly longer than those nuns who expressed themselves with fewer positive emotions.

This study shows that we should never stop engaging ourselves in cognitive activities if we want to lead a long and happy life. We should always workout or brain to keep it fit and healthy. Also, we should always strive to maintain a positive attitude towards life.

Rather than having a conventional mindset on retirement, you can work your way into finding the kind of work that you will never want to retire from.

"Choose a work that you love, and you won't have to work another day" - Confucius.

Retirement Is an Opportunity

Retirement is to be free of the responsibilities that we have when we work for money to make ends meet and to rediscover ourselves and do what we love.

It is an opportunity to do what you love to do, not for the money, nor to please anyone else. You can return to those things that make you happy and that give you meaning, but which you had to forgo because of your job or career.

Retirement should not mean an end to work. Rather it should just be a shift to a different kind of work. The kind of work that truly fulfills your purpose in life. The kind of work that you are born to do.

Chapter 12: The Preparation Gap

"I don't believe in luck; I believe in preparation" - Bobby Knight.

I am no big believer in luck the way that most people do. I don't buy lottery tickets and I don't gamble in the casinos. I don't believe in some overnight success or get-rich-quick schemes. Most people see luck as some external event that happens to them, and which is beyond their control. But to me luck is something which you have created intentionally over some time. Luck is your preparation manifesting into results. More than an event, luck is a process for me. I believe in what the Roman Philosopher Seneca once said, **"Luck is what happens when preparation meets opportunity"**, **or when** Samuel Goldwyn said, **"The harder I work the luckier I get"**.

Luck for me is like fishing. You know the fishes are there in the water, but you just can't sit beside the water and expect some fishes to jump out of the water and into your luck. I am not saying that it cannot happen. All I am saying is that the chances of that happening is very slim. Yet, that is exactly how most people view luck.

For me luck is like preparing oneself for fishing. You study all about the fishes - what they eat, when they eat, how big they are - and making the best tools to catch them. Once you have studied enough and put in enough effort in the process the actual catching of the fishes is not at all difficult. Rather it is fun. It may be elusive, but it is attainable. This is also one of the reasons why I enjoyed fishing a lot. It is like chasing your financial freedom. Elusive, but attainable.

See, opportunities, like fish, are always around the corner. It is for you to study where the opportunities are and hone your skills accordingly. It may take time for the preparation, but that is totally in your hand, in your control. Once prepared you can also maximize your opportunities by deliberately studying it and exposing yourself in those environments and places where you think are most opportunities.

Why Preparation Matters

"By failing to prepare you are preparing to fail" - Benjamin Franklin

Preparation is all the hard work and grindings that happen behind the scene. It is where the real actions take place. Most people are unaware of this side of the story as it remains mostly hidden. Also, most people don't want to know this side of the story. It is like the dark side of the moon. What people are only interested in is the results, the glory, and the outcome. People see the fruits of successful persons and expect themselves to be in that position without really wanting to know what goes on behind the curtain. This is the reason why most people will never succeed in life.

If you want success in life you have to prepare for it. You must be willing to pay the price. You have to undergo the process of hard work. The opportunity, when it presents itself, may not necessarily be the kind which you had expected, but it will be there. Opportunities are always there, all around us. Only the prepared minds will be able to see it when presented. The unprepared mind will not be able perceive it even when opportunities present itself. Even if he can perceive it, he still will not be able to receive it. If somehow, he can receive it, he still will not be able to keep it.

"Opportunity is a haughty goddess who wastes no time with those who are unprepared" - George S Clason.

Opportunities are also like radio-waves from a broadcast station. These waves are always there all around us, but you cannot receive them without a receiving device. The prepared mind is to opportunities as the receiving devices are to radio waves.

"It's better to be prepared for an opportunity and not have one than to have an opportunity and not be prepared"- Whitney M. Young

Preparation is a prerequisite for success. There are 'zero' people who are successful who do not work hard. But, don't get me wrong here. I am not saying that preparation is the only need for success. All I am saying is that it is a must. Apart from preparation one also needs focused attention, determination, desire, self-discipline etc.

Preparation also keeps us fit both mentally and physically. It also helps us endure any shortcomings or adversaries in our journey to success.

Abraham Lincoln is often quoted for having said, **"Give me six hours to chop down a tree and I will spend the first four sharpening the axe."** What Abraham Lincoln explains by this quote is that it is futile to take on any job without preparing for it first. It is crucial to take the time to think and get organized to ensure the efficiency and the success in any endeavor. If you rush though you risk making mistakes or wasting your time and energy. Before you do anything, you must learn as much as you can about the subject, get proper training, and be fully prepared. It may take longer and cost you more money, but you will save more time and money later.

As a kind of evolutionary survival mechanism, our brains are also hardwired for making quick judgments and reactions, that have helped us survive the plains of the savannah millions of years ago. But in today's modern, civilized world, we usually work on less life-threatening environments. Therefore, our impulse to leap before we look can sometimes do us more harm than good. If we want to work effectively and efficiently, we need to set careful goals and choose a wise strategy for reaching them. Otherwise, we are sure to waste precious resources.

As stated earlier, success is not an event or a place. It is a process - the path you travel towards your destination. It is the result of consistently putting in small quantities of daily efforts towards achieving your chief aim, your goal. Earl Nightingale once said **"Success really is nothing more than the progressive realization of a worthy goal or ideal. This means that any person who knows what they are doing is a success. Any person with a goal towards which they are working is a successful person"**. This is the best definition of success I've come across. Success is not the destination, but the journey. If you have a definite goal in life and if you are moving towards that goal you are a success.

'Be Prepared' is the motto of the Scout Movement used by millions of Scouts around the world since 1907. It means you are always in a state of readiness in mind and body to do your duty; Be Prepared in Mind by having disciplined yourself to be obedient to every order, and also by having thought out beforehand any accident or situation that might occur, so that you know the right thing to do at the right moment, and are willing to do it. Be Prepared in Body by making yourself strong and active and able to do the right thing at the right moment and do it. More than a century later, preparedness is still a cornerstone of Scouting. Through its fun, values-based program, Scouting prepares young people for life. Be Prepared is not just a concept, or a phrase to memorize. It is what we are all about. We are preparing our young generation for the future. We are instilling in them the values of preparedness and getting them ready to make good ethical and moral choices over their lifetimes. It is a good measure of getting ahead in life.

We humans tend to praise the results and outcomes, over the efforts and preparation. Most people equate preparing with 'not knowing your stuff.' However, this is a wrong approach. We must instead create a culture where how we get the results becomes as important as the result itself, and that preparing is something that the best leaders do to become even better. In the end it is who you become that matters. It's a competitive environment, and nobody can afford to not prepare. If you don't have to prepare for anything, that's a sign that you are not challenging yourself with new things. Preparation is one of the ways outstanding leaders drive results.

"What you get by achieving your goals is not as important as what you become by achieving your goals". - Henry David Thoreau.